Praise for

PROFIT
FIRST FOR
LAWYERS

I'm not a numbers person. I've never dealt with finances in my life! I don't even think as a young adult I balanced a checkbook right! I just lived on the Hope and Pray method, which is not the way to do it. *Profit First for Lawyers* specifically addresses the concerns and the issues that face law firm owners like me. It's a really good book for lawyers to read because it demystifies the numbers and gives us a different way of looking at profit.

~ Melissa Barry, *At Ease Law; Las Vegas, NV*

My first reaction after I finished reading *Profit First for Lawyers*, is that this is information that 99.9% of lawyers in the world have never heard before or even been exposed to. Most lawyers have never thought about their law firm in terms of their financials.

I would 100% recommend that every law firm owner in the country read *Profit First for Lawyers*. I promise you that no matter how long you have run your law firm or how profitable your law firm is, there is at least some nugget of wisdom in this book that will make your law firm a little bit more profitable.

~ Will Stafford, *Stafford Law Firm; Houston, TX*

Honestly, I'm not currently using Profit First accounting principles, but after reading *Profit First for Lawyers*, I'm definitely going to start. I know that's what I need to do to get to the next level. After reading this book, I realized there will never be anything left for me if I don't set it aside first. I know from seeing other people who have implemented *Profit First*, that it can work. And I just need to walk through my fear and do it.

~ Angela Klenk, *Beach Cities Estate Law; Torrance, CA*

I loved this book. I had purchased the original *Profit First*, and I wanted to read *Profit First for Lawyers* because it was tailored directly towards lawyers.

I found it to be a great supplement to the original *Profit First* book. It specifically goes into some of the reports we law firm owners need to go over on a regular basis. The main thing that I took away from the book were the last two chapters where RJon gave us the details we need to really dig into on a regular basis to make our law firms profitable.

~ MICHAEL REID, *M. Reid Legal Solutions; Clayton, MO*

I'm currently taking the teachings, the reporting, the metrics, the planning and everything in *Profit First for Lawyers*, and implementing it across my firm. And it's already making a positive impact! I just can't wait to see what it's going to do as I implement it fully.

~ ANDREA SHOUP, *Shoup Legal; Murrieta, CA*

I need to implement *profit first* because I didn't earn any money last year. I did not pay myself anything. I was living off of savings. While it is important to funnel money back into the business, *Profit First for Lawyers* taught me that I am a business owner, and part of being a business owner means I need to pay myself as well. I cannot continue to scrounge together the funds necessary to pay my mortgage, to pay my bills, to put food on the table. That money needs to be coming out of the business that I own rather than a constant cycle of draining my savings accounts.

~ NIKITA WOLF, *Wolf Law Center; Glen Allen, VA*

Profit First for Lawyers definitely helped me view my law firm differently. I feel more empowered as an entrepreneur. Every law firm owner should read it when they're starting up their own law firm. If I had had access to these concepts many years ago, there are definitely a lot of mistakes I wouldn't have made along the way.

~ LEAH MAYERSOHN, *Mayersohn Law Group; Ft. Lauderdale, FL*

Profit First for Lawyers definitely opened my eyes to how to run more of a profitable business. It outlined all the reports that I *should* be getting from an accountant or bookkeeper, and the different types of services that I should have in place to make sure that we are all rowing in the same direction. If you own a law firm and want to be more profitable, I would definitely recommend this book.

~ EDVIN FLORES, *Confianza Legal; Santa Fe Springs, CA*

PROFIT
FIRST FOR
LAWYERS

FREE BONUS:

Scan this QR code for a collection of tools, tips, and templates that you can use to make your law firm more profitable—before you even read the book!

PROFIT FIRST FOR LAWYERS

RJON ROBINS

TABLE OF CONTENTS

FOREWORD

by Mike Michalowicz, author of *Profit First*

The highly polished, mirror-like finish meant one thing to me. It was brand new.

This was the first time I set my eyes on the fabled Tesla S1 sedan. The color was fire-engine red, nonetheless. Tesla had been manufacturing it for years, but now I was seeing it in the flesh, so to speak. If you are not familiar with this car's capabilities, it is faster than every other production car in the world. Bar none. It leaves Ferraris, Porsches, and Corvettes in the dust. To add insult to injury, it does it with the unignorable sound of silence.

No oversized gasoline engine. No guttural exhaust notes. No clunky gear shifting. Just constant, uncontestable, electric power.

"Hop in!" RJon told me excitedly.

The interior was as polished and pristine as the body's paint. I sunk into the passenger seat and latched the seat belt. I tugged it twice to ensure it was properly secured. Okay, not twice, more like four times.

"I hear these things are pretty fast," I side-mouthed to RJon with my eyes locked on the straightway in front of us.

"Yes, it's powerful. It's fun. And it's safe," he responded. "It lets me do things I couldn't do before in a car. This car has changed the way that I drive." Then, he said, "Buckle up, buttercup. Here we go!"

It was somewhere between the phrases "Buckle up buttercup" and "Here we go" that he had mashed the pedal. I was instantly pinned against the seat. The only sound was a whir, yet the powerful g-force was instant and persistent—only something I can compare to an extreme roller coaster launch. I glanced down at the speedometer as he finished saying, "Here we go."

By the last word, we had surpassed 60 miles per hour. A blink later, we were at 100 mph. Undeniable power. Available instantly.

RJon took his foot off the accelerator, and the car came to a spirited stop. My seat belt remained secure, but my heart was now racing. RJon turned to me, smiled, and said, "Your turn."

In those few minutes behind the wheel, grinning ear-to-ear, I gained a whole new understanding of power. While history had taught me that gasoline equates to power, I now had an experience of something new. Something stronger, faster, and cleaner. I realized that just because something has been around for a long, long time doesn't mean it's the best.

Profit First, in my opinion, is an electric innovation. It challenges the notion of oversized cash management strategies, exhausted budgeting approaches, and clunky accounting principles. It introduces a radically simple system that accelerates profit with undeniable power, safety, and speed. And RJon Robins is the perfect person to take you and your law firm for this ride of a lifetime.

RJon is undeniably successful. He comes from financial struggle—scrounging to pay groceries and facing foreclosure—to American-dream status. Today he's the founder of a $30 million dollar business that's been named by *Inc.* Magazine as one of the fastest growing privately held companies in the country every year in a row since 2015 and which employs more than 150 amazing people. RJon has personally coached, counseled, advised, and kicked the butts of many thousands of law firm owners. As a result, he is the one common denominator behind more rags-to-riches, multimillion-dollar law firms than anyone else on the planet. That is not hyperbole. That is fact.

A lawyer himself, he is an active member of the Florida Bar and a certified Profit First Professional. Amongst RJon's portfolio of companies serving entrepreneurial small law firm owners is a bookkeeping company called "Small Law Firm Bookkeeping That Does NOT Suck." Yes, that's really the name. As of this writing, Small Law Firm Bookkeeping That Does NOT Suck is the largest and fastest-growing bookkeeping business in the country dedicated exclusively to the unique challenges faced by fast-growing small law firms.

And in his other business, How To Manage A Small Law Firm, RJon's team of small law firm management professionals helps manage nearly one thousand of the fastest-growing and most profitable law firms I thought I'd ever meet. In other words, RJon knows the business of law firms, and he knows how to make them permanently profitable. So, you can leverage the lessons, strategies, and practical tactics he is about to share with you in the book—big time.

But why reveal all he knows right in this book? Just like RJon's Tesla has forever changed his approach to driving (and my appreciation of power), Profit First principles have changed the way he manages his business. And I've known RJon long enough to know that he believes in "paying it forward." That's exactly what RJon is doing for you in *Profit First for Lawyers*.

This book is your steering wheel to permanent profitability. So, set the dial to "ludicrous" speed, grab the wheel, and hover your foot above the accelerator. Are you nervous or even a bit scared? Don't worry, RJon is riding shotgun with you.

Buckle up, buttercup. Here we go. Mash it down.

■ ■ ■

PART I

CHAPTER 1

THIS BOOK WILL MAKE YOUR LAW FIRM MORE PROFITABLE

This book will make your law firm more profitable. It may also piss you off. This book is meant to be a rallying cry for entrepreneurially minded small law firm owners everywhere. This book is dedicated to you if you are committed to finding a better way to grow your business and a better way to live your life.

If you implement what's explained in this book, your law firm will *definitely* become more profitable. You will feel more confidence. And you will begin to experience the unique satisfaction that comes from being able to put more of the revenue collected by your law firm into your own personal bank account reliably every month and quarter. These are my promises to you—as author to reader.

You will notice that I used the word "will" throughout the paragraph above. No hedge words. I promise you that these desirable effects will begin to show up in your law firm and in your life as soon as you put into action—and in proportion to the effort you expend taking action on—the causes that I will explain in plain English throughout this book.

Yes, it's true. One day, not long from now, you will wake up to find that you are taking more profits from your law firm:

1. Without having to do any more marketing or taking on any more clients than your law firm already serves—though you may find the confidence you've been looking for to decline some of your firm's less-desirable clients;

2. Without having to hire more staff—though you may have to replace some current staff and vendors when you read chapter 14; and

3. Without having to increase overhead.

And reliably! Did I mention reliably? Not only will your law firm become more profitable, but also its profits will flow to you more reliably—and in more ways than just financially speaking.

But when you discover the culprits who have been keeping you separated from your profits, it will probably piss you off. At first, you may find yourself in a state of denial:

- "This can't be."

- "It couldn't be this simple."

- "They're supposed to be looking out for me!"

But your personal bank account(s) will be growing right before your eyes. And your worries about cash flow will begin to subside. And one day, you'll probably wake up pretty pissed off about all the bad advice you may have paid for and followed over the years that kept you from your profits—or rather kept your profits away from you!

But to deliver on my promises to you, we are going to have to work together. I'm going to be asking you to keep an open mind about the merits of some of the "conventional wisdom" you've probably been taught about the business of how to manage a small law firm. If you want to produce unconventionally desirable results, you can't rely on conventional wisdom and just do what everyone else does. So, thank you in advance for keeping an open mind. Once you understand my reasons, it will be much easier for you to take some of the steps I'm going to ask you to take throughout this book.

CONVENTIONAL THINKING =

CONVENTIONAL RESULTS

UNCONVENTIONALLY PROFITABLE RESULTS

(REQUIRE) UNCONVENTIONAL THINKING

WHAT IF I'VE ALREADY READ *PROFIT FIRST* BY MIKE MICHALOWICZ? (AND WHAT IF I HAVEN'T?)

This book is not a replacement for reading (or listening to) *Profit First* by my friend Mike Michalowicz, who asked me to write this book for the legal industry. Mike asked me to write a book like this after he visited one of our now-famous Live Quarterly Meetings. That's where he first met hundreds and hundreds of small law firm owners whose businesses my own firm helps manage and grow. Mike saw how they were very happily, very profitably, and very UN-conventionally applying *Profit First* to make their law firms more profitable and improve their lives in other important ways, too.

So, you don't have to worry. This won't be a cheap "find and replace" job. I hate it when authors write an "industry-specific" version of their already popular book and simply perform a "find and replace" function; talk about a cop-out! Instead, this book is meant to get you to read or listen to the original *Profit First* (if you haven't already) and implement the Profit First principles in your law firm if you are not already using them.

GOOD NEWS: If you are already using *Profit First* in your law firm, you will probably enjoy the deeper discussions that take place within this book that are more specific to the legal industry. And you will profit even more from the additional resources I will share to help you get even more profit out of your law firm. Plus, we'll be able to get into more detail about why and how to make Profit First work ESPECIALLY WELL for a law firm, in ways that Mike could not fully explore—because the original book is obviously aimed at a wider audience than just small law firm owners.

BETTER NEWS: If you have read but not yet fully embraced Profit First in your law firm (perhaps due to a lack of support from your book-keeper, tax strategist, or C.P.A.), this book will give you the tools that you may need to fight for your right to make it a priority that your law firm remains or becomes a profit-breathing machine. You owe it to your *clients* to run a profitable law firm. Yes, we'll explore this concept more fully later in this book too: Why You Have an Ethical & a Professional Responsibility to Run a Profitable Law Firm! And why lawyers who allow their clients to hire unprofitable law firms do those clients a disservice. I'll argue later in the book why and how that's even a violation of Bar rules in most states!

DON'T WORRY: If you have not yet read (or listened to) *Profit First*, I'll explain enough about that book throughout this one, so you won't be lost. **If you haven't read (or listened to) the original book, I recommend that you do.** As I said, this isn't just a  regurgitation of that book. This is a wholly new book. They will complement each other—no matter which you read (or listen to) first.

Together, the two books will equip you to be an effective advocate for yourself, even if you do make the very smart decision to seek out a Profit

First Certified Professional Bookkeeper to help you. Becoming familiar with the original source material will make your job of managing and working with your bookkeeper, C.P.A., and/or tax strategist that much more profitable *for you*!

Go to www.ProfitFirstForLawyers.com/ResourceBundle or follow this QR Code for additional resources and some bonus "behind the scenes" content you can use to begin making your law firm more profitable right away.

As we near the end of our first chapter together and because I know you don't know me very well yet, I'll break this to you gently:

Your Accountant, Bookkeeper, and/or C.P.A. Probably
Don't Want You to Read This Book.

It's not because they begrudge you for your profits. Instead, it's probably because they're just unfamiliar with the principles of Profit First. Implementing these simple, yet effective principles requires an accountant, a bookkeeper, and/or your C.P.A. to work "differently" than how they've been trained and indoctrinated—often without even thinking about why. Implementing Profit First requires us to do things in a way that is not contemplated by Generally Accepted Accounting Principles (GAAP). And too many C.P.A.s regard GAAP as gospel—and it isn't.

So, a lot of what you're going to learn from reading or listening to *Profit First* and by reading or listening to this book challenges the conventional wisdom that many of your financial advisors are familiar (and therefore comfortable) with. And sadly, most people would prefer to adapt themselves to the demands of an unprofitable business rather than challenge conventional thinking and leave their comfort zone—even if doing so makes their business more profitable and helps more clients.

All of this is to say I know I have my work cut out for me in this book. I not only have to PROVE TO YOU that Profit First works for law firms, but I must also educate you enough and equip you with sufficient proof to help you withstand the onslaught of doubt your own bookkeeper, tax strategist, and/or C.P.A. will likely throw at you when you announce: "I'm Going to Take My Profits First!"

Unless, of course, you're already working with a Certified Profit First Professional.

Or at least a professional advisor who is open-minded enough to consider that there "could" be a better way to help you maximize the profits you take from your law firm. After all, isn't that one of the main reasons you pay these people? (That's a rhetorical question.)

If it was your bookkeeper, tax strategist, or C.P.A. (or someone else) who recommended you read this book, please take a moment right now to let me know who that person is who cares so much about you. **I want to send that person a thank you note** (no joke)! Visit: www.ProfitFirstForLawyers.com/ThankYouNote, or scan the QR code below.

. . .

CHAPTER 2

YOU ARE NOT ALONE

GOOD NEWS: YOU ARE NOT ALONE.

OR AT LEAST, YOU DON'T HAVE TO BE.

I*'ve learned the lessons contained in this book* the hard way myself. I'm not writing this book from some ivory tower. In fact, in 2009, I was flat broke. Sure, I rose from the ashes like a phoenix and built my business into a profitable, multiple-eight-figure enterprise, which today gives me the freedom to live life on my terms. But I didn't do it without a lot of help. I've accumulated more than my fair share of scars, bruises, and bumps along the way. And part of why I agreed to write this book is to spare you some of the pain I experienced.

By the time you are done reading this book, you are going to feel more empowered and have more confidence when you break it to your bookkeeper, tax strategist, or C.P.A. and perhaps even your business partner(s) that you are going to stop allowing your law firm's fullest potential to be held hostage by conventional wisdom and begin making the profitability of your law firm one of your top priorities.

To be fair, implementing Profit First for a small law firm isn't as convenient or familiar for a bookkeeper, tax strategist, or C.P.A. as NOT implementing Profit First. So, you must decide what's more important for you: the comfort and convenience of your professional advisors OR the profitability of your business. Keep in mind, the profitability of your business benefits your law firm's clients, its staff, and your family, too, who have a lot riding on the profitability of your law firm. So, what's it going to be?

Sorry to pile on, but to further complicate the conversation, you should know that by the time you're done reading this book you will be willing—even *happy*—to pay more for your professionals to go the extra mile and implement Profit First for your law firm, which will generate more revenue to *their* business, too. You will see that by paying (investing) a little bit more to have your bookkeeper, C.P.A., and/or tax strategist implement Profit First in your law firm, it will put a lot more profit into your personal bank account. It is at this point when you may feel like you're all alone and losing your mind when some of your professional advisors push back and essentially say to you: *"No! Pay me less, so that I can do less for you. That way, we can BOTH make less profit."*

But you're not alone. Thousands of small law firm owners have had this same *Twilight Zone* conversation with their bookkeepers, tax strategists, C.P.A.s, and even their own law firm business partners! So, if you find your blood pressure rising while you're reading this book; if it's beginning to dawn on you just how much profit you have been leaving on the table and for how long, simply because your bookkeeper or your accountant couldn't be bothered to do things a little bit differently than they "normally" do . . . all I can say at this point is this: Aren't you glad you're reading this book TODAY instead of ten years from now?

In all seriousness, **you're not alone, and if you want to see even more proof that you're not alone, be sure to visit www.ProfitFirstForLawyers.com /AmICrazy or scan this QR code** to see an ever-growing collection of sometimes funny, sometimes  heartbreaking stories of law firm owners who felt all alone until we discovered each other. The reality is that if you own a law firm and your family's well-being depends on the income you earn from your law firm, then this book should get you really excited about the possibilities. Even if you don't care about your family but you care about your clients and recognize that their well-being depends on your law firm to be profitable so that you and your staff can "show up" as the best version of yourselves, then this book should still get you really excited about the possibilities.

"But RJon, what if I don't care about my family and I don't care about my clients or my staff, and I'm not willing to challenge my bookkeeper or accountant if they give me any pushback about implementing Profit First? Should I still read this book?"

No. If that's where your mindset is at, you should stop reading this book right now and just go chew some gum.

By reading this book and implementing Profit First, you are going to discover how to unlock tremendous profits that are trapped in your business:

- With ZERO additional marketing;

- No new clients; and

- No additional legal production work needed from you or your staff.

You'll be able to work less and profit more.

I know that probably sounds "too good to be true." But I will show you proof that it's possible—and that it can happen much more quickly than you probably realize. In fact, if you're willing to apply what you learn in this book, you can wake up 30 days from now enjoying the many benefits of owning a much more reliably profitable law firm.

But don't just take my word for it . . .

"The biggest thing about Profit First was that it decluttered all the numbers in my mind and made everything very simple to look at. . . I can clearly see what's happening in my firm, and I can now plan-ahead so I'm not surprised by cash-flow gaps or other speed bumps."

Susan Katzen ◆ Newport Beach, CA
SKatzenLaw.com

"Profit First opened my eyes to a way to be in control of my financials and make more money. Implementing the lessons learned after fully understanding them was the key to helping me simplify my financials so that I could enjoy my business. It's time to LOVE YOUR NUMBERS so they don't stress you out and control you. Take back control!"

Kim Benjamin ◆ Kansas City, MO
DWICriminalLawCenter.com

"I had no system before Profit First. Money came in, and money went out. I didn't know what I needed to do. I'd receive a credit card bill, and then my whole focus had to shift over to how to pay it. It was all very tactical from month-to-month. Profit First got me out of that because I was able to learn about and implement a financial strategy and changed (improved) my mindset toward money. That got us out of $100,000 of debt within about one year of implementing Profit First. It's a better way to run a law firm and a better way to live, for sure."

Kishore Kapoor ◆ Hamden, CT
ConnecticutRealEstateClosingAttorneys.com

"With very little effort, Profit First has made a huge, positive difference in my life. For years, I got paid last, making less in my own firm than I would working for someone else. I got what was left over after all other expenses. With Profit First, I first pay myself my hard earned profit every month. My total owner benefit has increased by over 300%. I also set money aside monthly for cash reserves and income taxes – so no more worrying about being unprepared for surprises."

Margaret Barrett ✦ St. Paul, MN
SafeHarborEstateLaw.com

"After implementing Profit First in late September, I was able to take home 33% more profit from my law firm, in just the last quarter of the year. That's how fast this can produce results."

Samuel Doncaster ✦ Phoenix, AZ
FraudFightersLawFirm.com

"When I started my business, I ran its finances like I ran my personal finances: If I had money in the bank, I spent it. And when it came time to take a distribution, I wondered where the money went. I was essentially living on W-2 income, wondering why I wasn't wealthier after working so hard in the business. After implementing Profit First, I set aside 10% of my business' gross monthly income and run it with the remaining 90%. Amazingly, expenses "fit" inside that 90%. And, best of all, I can take a distribution of that 10% of gross (if not more) whenever I want – because I paid myself first!"

Todd M. Wesche ✦ Boston, MA
VetusLegal.com

CHAPTER 3

MY DEFINITION OF A SUCCESSFUL LAW FIRM

(And Why It Should Be Yours, Too)

To *begin with, I should tell you* that I have been working almost exclusively with solo and small law firm owners since August 24, 1999. That was the day I first reported for duty as a Small Law Practice Management Advisor with the Florida Bar's Law Office Management Assistance Service (LOMAS).

By the time I left four years later, I'd had the unique opportunity to help THOUSANDS of solo and small law firm owners with just about every law firm management challenge (and plenty of opportunities) I could ever imagine. I thought I'd earned the equivalent of an M.B.A. from The School of Hard Knocks.

But I was wrong.

Later, after I left LOMAS, my wife became seriously ill. And since I had (foolishly) failed to follow my own (excellent) advice about why and how to put profits first and how to manage a successful business, we ended up losing our home to foreclosure and went broke in 2009. This happened mostly because I had unwittingly settled for having a very nice practice but hadn't created a sustainable business that could operate without me. It was then that I realized I had NOT actually earned an M.B.A. from The School of Hard Knocks and that the previous 10 years' experience of helping thousands of small law firm owners start, market, manage, and grow thousands of different kinds of law firms and avoid the exact mistake I'd so foolishly made myself . . . that was all just the entrance exam!

Today, How To Manage A Small Law Firm—the firm I co-founded with my wife after her recovery—helps manage more than 600 of some of the most successful, fastest-growing, most fun-to-run, and highly profitable solo and small law firms across the United States. We even help to manage some small law firms in a few other countries. The law firms we choose to work with are being run by entrepreneurs who are also lawyers. They come to us from all walks of life and own firms that provide solutions for clients in every area of the law you can probably imagine.

We help these business owners by stepping in and functioning as their Law Firm Business Management Advisor. And, in some cases, we function as a "timeshare" CEO, COO, CFO, and/or CMO for the law firm, too, until the firm grows to a point where it's feasible or necessary to bring these important business management positions in-house, full-time for the law firm. Then, we help them do just that!

Yes. Your law firm is a law firm. It is also a business. Presumably, it is a business you started with at least one of the goals being to create a better future for yourself and your family. With as many small law firm owners as I've spoken with over the years, I've never met a single lawyer who said (or would admit) that their goal was to have an "unsuccessful" business. Instead, everyone says they want their law firm to be successful. And why wouldn't you want your firm to be successful? In fact, why wouldn't you want it to be as successful as it can possibly be? To want your law firm to be less than all it can be is abnormal—especially when you consider that at least part of a law firm's success is dependent upon the law firm helping more people.

It's true! All things being equal, a million-dollar law firm *becomes* a million-dollar law firm because it helps twice as many people as a half-million-dollar law firm. Just as a half-million-dollar law firm becomes a half-million-dollar law firm by helping twice as many people as a law firm grossing a quarter-million dollars. Or if the higher-grossing firm isn't helping twice as many clients, then it's likely providing twice as much value to the same number of clients. How else could it be grossing twice as much? Plenty of broke and struggling law firm owners are willing to waste their time arguing this point. But you already know these are true statements because you know the way all well-run professional service firms generate revenue is by:

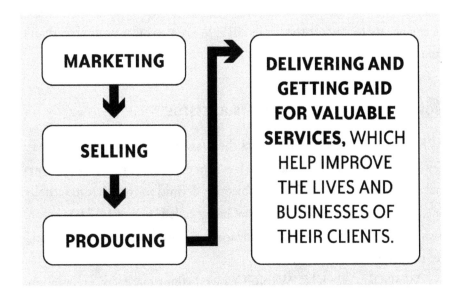

MARKETING

SELLING

PRODUCING

DELIVERING AND GETTING PAID FOR VALUABLE SERVICES, WHICH HELP IMPROVE THE LIVES AND BUSINESSES OF THEIR CLIENTS.

And while you can fool some of the people some of the time, you can't fool all the people all the time. So, that is how you know that any time you see a professional services firm with successive years of growth-on-growth, it's a pretty good barometer of how much VALUE the firm is producing in the lives and/or businesses of its clients.

Notice that I didn't say any of this is a good barometer of how much PROFIT the Owner or Owners of the firm are enjoying. That's because gross revenue is only a barometer of how much value is being delivered. Making sure your growing law firm is also profitable—that's a different story. And it is a story we are going to concern ourselves with throughout the remaining chapters of this book!

Now would probably be a good time for me to mention that since its founding at my kitchen table (literally), How To Manage A Small Law Firm has grown to become the largest and the fastest-growing company of its kind, focused exclusively on helping manage small law firms. No, it's not a terribly creative name, but How To Manage A Small Law Firm has been named by *Inc.* Magazine as a "Best Place to Work"; and we've made it to the INC 5000 List of Fastest-Growing Companies year-over-year since we first made the list in 2015. We're also quite profitable, thank you very much.

HOW TO KNOW IF A LAW FIRM IS "SUCCESSFUL"

While every law firm owner wants their law firm to be "successful," very few out of the tens of thousands of law firm owners I've met over the years have been able to articulate an objective definition for what it actually means for a law firm to be worthy of being called "successful." But before I share my definition of what it means for a law firm to be "successful," let me ask you a question:

Would you ever KNOWINGLY invest your time, energy, reputation, money, and credit and make impositions on your family for a business that you knew going into it couldn't, wouldn't, or was at the very least unlikely to make a financial profit?

Why not?

Isn't the short version of your answer, "Because that would be just crazy"?

■ ■ ■

CHAPTER 4

"BUT FINANCIAL PROFIT ISN'T THE ONLY MEASURE OF SUCCESS!"

This *is what all the broke* and struggling law firm owners always say—quite predictably.

And they're right.

Just as the front left wheel of your car isn't the only wheel on your car. There are three other wheels that are equally important. But without that front left wheel, you're going nowhere, fast.

No rational person starts a business with the intention of it not being a financially viable venture. And without financial viability, even the most noble business started with the best of intentions will soon be out of business and of no use to anyone. The rational person starts a business typically by investing time, energy, and some risk capital with the intention of realizing a positive financial return on these investments. Not only is this your moral right, but it's also a practical necessity! Keep in mind that even nonprofits must generate a positive ROI. They simply distribute their profits in the form of additional services to their constituents instead of to their shareholders. But your family didn't agree to invest in a nonprofit, did they?

So, here's my definition of what it means for a law firm to be worthy of being called a "successful" business. See if this helps give you an objective criterion—or at least a way to arrive at an objective criterion for evaluating how "successful" your law firm is, or any other law firm:

1. Financially Successful: To be deemed a "financially successful business," the law firm must generate enough Total Owner Benefits (an important term we'll explore later in this book) to afford its Owner the opportunity to live the way they want to live. Not just the way the Owner(s) are willing to "settle" for living; not to live merely with what they can "make do" with. To be called a "financially successful business," a law firm must generate enough Total Owner Benefits, and therefore financial profits, for an Owner to live the way they want to live. Otherwise, it's just a hobby.

2. Personally Successful: To the extent that a law firm operates with sufficiently robust systems that it gives its Owner(s) the freedom of time to attend to every aspect of their life and doesn't just require the Owner to be a servant to the law firm, that is the extent to which we can say a law firm is "Personally Successful." If the only way for a law firm to generate enough net operating income for the Owner to live the way they want to live in terms of material possessions is for the Owner to be a slave to their law firm, that's not a fully successful business. Not in my book. (Get it? ☺)

   We measure the Personal Success of a law firm by the number of consecutive days, weeks, and months that the business can meet its legal, ethical, professional, and financial obligations, including its financial obligations to the Owner even while the Owner is away, with defined "Emergency Access Only."

   The law firm that cannot function without its Owner(s) being there every day is a "practice" or a "job," not a sustainable business.

3. Professionally Successful: Law firms generate revenue by helping people solve their problems and create a better future for their clients. Lawyers tend to choose to start firms in the practice area(s) they choose because there's often something about the world that the lawyer feels they're improving through that area of the law, which is meaningful for the Owner of the law firm. Sometimes this centers around a type of client-avatar the law firm is set up to help. Other times, the firm is dedicated to help solve one or more problems in the world that the Owner cares about improving. And sometimes, it is both.

     We can devise simple and objective systems for measuring the positive impact that a law firm's operations have in the world. This measurement tends to be a reliable indicator of how "Professionally Successful" the law firm is. As a simple example: "Have we helped more clients this quarter than we helped last quarter?"

SOME WORDS OF ENCOURAGEMENT:

This doesn't have to be overwhelming. Not if we break it down to The 7 Main Parts™.

See if this helps:

A law firm is a business. As such, it has just 7 Main Parts. That's right, there are only 7 Main Parts of every Successful Law Firm™. They're the same 7 Main Parts as every unsuccessful law firm, too. The difference between the successful law firms and the law firms that struggle is the degree to which the Owner(s) of the firm are aware of, attend to, and keep each of the 7 Main Parts in alignment. Otherwise, the firm's "throughput" winds up functioning a lot like a garden hose with one or more kinks in it. Consider each of the following all-too-common scenarios:

- **Great Marketing, Bad Sales:** This firm's cost of acquiring new clients will be higher than necessary, and the firm will be producing a lot of frustrated prospective new clients who will spread the word about the firm's lack of responsiveness, which will tend to drive up marketing costs and suck profits.

- **Great Marketing & Sales, But Not Enough Staff:** This type of firm will have an unprofitable backlog of work, frustrated clients, costly refunds, some "close calls," and eventually, some Bar complaints, too. Keep in mind that the quickest way to sink a poorly managed business is with great marketing!

- **The Most Amazing Lawyers and Dedicated Staff, but Bad or Simply "Inconsistent" or "Unplanned" Marketing:** These law firms experience "Feast or Famine" cash flow, and management will tend to begin accepting less-than-ideal clients or cases to address short-term cash-flow challenges. This is actually where the MOST Bar grievances come from.

- **Great Marketing, Great Sales, and Great Staff, but Unclear Internal Workflow Processes, Inadequate Ongoing Training, and/or Out-Of-Date Equipment:** In this environment, we find elevated levels of staff frustration, depressed career satisfaction, and expensive (profit-sucking) turnover.

- **Everything Is Just Absolutely Amazing, and You Have the Potential to Be the Best Lawyer in the Whole Wide World, but Your Firm Lacks Adequate Financial Controls.** Anytime there is unrealized potential, there is frustration. Sadly (my editor wants me to use the word "tragically," but I'm going to go with the word sadly), there are too many great lawyers with loads of potential but not enough profits to invest in more consistent marketing or more professional sales systems. Too many of these great lawyers are frustrated and cannot live up to their full potential because their law firms lack profits enough to hire the best staff, provide ongoing training to keep their staff at the top of their game, and equip the firm with the latest and best tools so everyone can work at maximum efficiency. The lawyers who own these types of law firms often show up as an emotional wreck after having to break the news to their family that they can't afford to give them the lives they (you) desperately want to be able to provide.

On second thought, that is pretty tragic, don't you think?

Profit First solves most of these problems. Or rather, implementing Profit First gives you the tools (profits) with which to solve most of these problems.

Keep in mind, there are only three reasons why some law firms are successful while others in the same practice area and even in the same marketplace are not (more on that in a moment). So, when we "pop open the hood" in struggling law firms, we find one or more of The 7 Main Parts™ have been left unattended. Often this is not the fault of the lawyer(s) who own the law firm. After all, what did they teach any of us in law school about the BUSINESS of running a law firm? (This is another rhetorical question.)

If your law school experience was anything like mine or that of the many hundreds and hundreds of now-successful small law firm owners we work with at How To Manage A Small Law Firm, chances are they taught you NOTHING in law school about the business of how to manage a law firm.

In fact, they may have even given you the same bad advice I've heard repeated from the many thousands of lawyers I've had the opportunity to work with over the years: "Just be a good lawyer, and the rest will take care of itself."

Yeah, right. As if there are some magic law firm management elves who are going to come into your law firm at night or over the weekends when you're not there and attend to the marketing and sales and think through and document workflow processes. Then, they'll read your mind and create job descriptions and internal training programs, plan for the physical plant needs of your growing law firm, and install, monitor, and make well-informed decisions for you based on grown-up financial controls. And why, pray tell, will those magic law firm management elves do all of this for you? To reward you for being such a good lawyer, of course!

More lawyers than you might imagine actually believe this fairy tale. Mostly because they want to. Unfortunately, the widespread belief in this fairy tale in the legal profession leads to a lot of guilt and shame and embarrassment. Because great lawyers who care deeply for their clients and their causes but who have never taken even a single course in their life about the business of how to manage a small law firm wind up with predictably bad results.

Their law firms aren't financially successful because there are no marketing budgets, no pricing strategies, no business efficiencies, and no financial controls.

Their law firms aren't personally successful because there are no workflow processes, no operating policies, and no instructive procedures for anyone to follow while the Owner(s) are away.

Inevitably, the law firm falls far short of its potential for professional success, too, because the business can't achieve any kind of scale. It can't gain any kind of real momentum. And the Owner(s) are always operating at less than their best due to overwork, not enough staff to help them, uncertainties about cash flow, and too much stress and anxiety about the future.

And then, of course, comes a scene you're probably already all too familiar with. These well-intentioned law firm owners show up at their local Bar function where they're surrounded by help-rejecting complainers who take pride in, and actually brag about, all their problems.

And no one is willing to speak openly about the real cause of the problems you can be sure most law firm owners you know are likely struggling with: They're running a BUSINESS with no business plan.

This is a lot like taking a case to trial with no trial plan. Or conducting a complex transaction with no work plan. Or playing blind archery. Pick whichever analogy resonates most with you as being the most likely to produce predictably bad results:

POP QUIZ

1. What sort of bad thing would you expect to happen in a law firm with no real marketing plan? That is, no overarching strategy, no marketing budget, no metrics, and no one holding anyone accountable for any of the money being spent?

2. How much stress would you expect the Owner(s) of a law firm to have that has no sales system that can reliably qualify/disqualify and convert prospective new clients into paying clients of the firm, even when the Owner(s) are away?

3. How many avoidable arguments can you imagine the Owner(s) of a small law firm having with their family who is waiting for them at home, when the Owner is stuck at the office having to do everything themselves because the firm lacks any sort of documented, delegable, and/or manageable systems for producing the work?

BONUS POINT: Earn a bonus point if you can correctly answer the question: "How do you KNOW this affects the quality of the Owner(s)' work?"

POP QUIZ

4. How many hundreds of thousands of dollars do you expect are likely being wasted in a small law firm where no one has ever bothered to create clear, objective job descriptions, key performance indicators, and/or ongoing training programs for getting, keeping, and maximizing staff performance?

5. What do you expect would be the top three headaches experienced by Owners of small law firms where there are no plans or strategic thinking being done with regard to the physical plant needs for a growing law firm?

6. By what percentage could you easily imagine the profitability of a small law firm improving when the Owner(s) go from having no financial controls and no real plans for how to be sure to take profits predictably from the law firm ... to having proper financial controls and a plan to implement Profit First?

BONUS OPPORTUNITY: Take this quiz online, and if you get a "B+" or better, you will get the opportunity to choose a prize (one of which may or may not be a free pony)!

On a scale of 1–10 (with 10 being the most), exactly how self-defeating would you say it would be for the Owner of any kind of business (yes, even a law firm) to wake up every day and go to work without the benefit of having any sort of clear financial, personal, and/or professional goals against which the success of the business can be measured and course-corrected when called for?

OK, now all joking aside (except I'm not joking about the free pony—I never joke about free ponies), all your answers for the pop quiz are pretty bad, right?

Now here come the words of encouragement:

It Doesn't Have to Be Like This for You.

To summarize everything you've just read:

The First Reason so many small law firms struggle to become or remain profitable is lack of education, or rather lack of education about the business of how to manage a successful small law firm. The lawyer or lawyers who own the business simply don't know enough about how to manage the business of the law firm and often exacerbate the problem by working harder, but on the wrong things.

The Second Reason why law firms struggle is mismanagement and inattention. The lawyer may know what to do but fails to find the time to build proper business operational processes, policies, procedures, and systems. This can be the most frustrating of all three reasons because in this instance, the lawyer "knows better" but simply cannot find the time to "do better." And until the law firm achieves enough scale to bring in full-time experienced law firm management professionals, the firm just sort of stumbles along.

The Third Reason why law firms struggle to realize their fullest potential is mindset—how the Owner(s) think about what they think about, the excuses they make, the excuses they accept, the unexamined stories they take as gospel. Henry Ford once said, "No matter if you think you can or think you can't, you're [going to find a way to be] right." Implementing Profit First makes it impossible to think that your law firm cannot be more profitable because instantly, it will be!

■ ■ ■

CHAPTER 5

THE 7 MAIN PARTS OF EVERY SUCCESSFUL LAW FIRM

I *have a question that I have posed* to literally tens of thousands of small law firm owners: What is the business of a law firm?

The answers I would get most often were, "to enforce the law," "to protect people's rights," "to make clients happy." But that's *not* the business of a law firm; that's the job of the lawyer.

So I would say, "let's change gears. What's the business of a restaurant? What's the business of a hotel?" And pretty soon they would start to understand.

What's the business of a restaurant? To sell food.

What's the business of a hotel? To rent rooms.

The *strategy* of how they go about selling food and renting rooms is going to be different restaurant-to-restaurant, and hotel-to-hotel, but at the end of the day *all* restaurants are in the business of selling food, and *all* hotels are in the business of renting rooms.

So, the business of a law firm is quite simply to sell and deliver legal services. The job of the *lawyer* is to deliver amazing and life-changing services like standing up for and defending people's rights, enforcing the law, ensuring justice is served, etc. But the business of a law firm is very simple. You have to market; you have to sell; you have to produce; you have to deliver; and you have to get paid for your work.

Every small law firm needs a written business plan that explains in plain English how the firm is supposed to work and generate a profit. Central to this business plan, which must be revised and revamped about every 12–18 months, are the personal, professional, and financial goals of the owner, which the firm needs to provide for—or else, what's the point of it all? The problem is most small law firm owners never went to business school, so the idea of writing a business plan is daunting and intimidating, but it doesn't have to be once we simplify it and break it down to The 7 Main Parts of a Successful Law Firm™. And yes, **there are only 7 Main Parts in every successful law firm** (and in every unsuccessful law firm, too).

What makes a law firm successful is how well each of these parts is working and whether each of them is aligned with the goals of the firm, which are designed in the law firm's business plan. Writing that business plan doesn't have to be complicated; it just needs to paint a picture of how the firm will work and how The 7 Main Parts work together to achieve the goals of the firm. So, let me define each of these parts.

PART 1: MARKETING

Marketing is everything that gets done to bring the *right* kind of prospective new clients to the door at the right time, in the right quantity, and in the right frame of mind. But marketing should not only act as a magnet that attracts the right kind of client to your firm; it should also act as a magnet that repels the *wrong* kind of client away from your firm. This protects you, it protects your staff, and it demonstrates respect for the prospective new client by preventing them from wasting their time pursuing your firm if you already know that they're not the right client for you or they don't have the right kind of case for your firm.

PART 2: SALES

The second main part of every successful law firm is the Sales Process. When done the right way, sales is one of the most thoughtful, caring, considerate, and I'll even go so far as to say loving things you can do for another person. In business, sales is nothing more than helping a person make sense of their situation, find clarity about their options, and then helping them make an educated, informed decision about what they want to do next. Sales is a service you do *for* another person, not *to* them.

Your sales process should be structured in a systematic, organized, consistent, predictable, ethical, and replicable way. Ideally in a way that could be done by someone who's not even an attorney! At How To Manage A Small Law Firm, we call non-attorney salespeople "Dragons," and when they're properly trained to provide consultations to your prospective new clients—*not legal advice!*—they free you (or the other attorneys in your office) from having to stop doing legal work to meet with a prospect. Additionally, the non-attorney salesperson can meet with prospective new clients while you're out of the office so that when you come back from vacation, you find your business making more money than when you left it. Finally, when you have your marketing functioning effectively, a good Dragon should be converting at a higher rate than you can—this hurts the ego of some small law firm owners; but at the end of the day, if what you want is results, hiring a non-attorney salesperson that does nothing but sell your firm's legal services all day is the way to go.

PART 3: PRODUCTION

The third main part of every successful law firm is the Production: documented processes, systems, and procedures for how the work in the firm gets done. Meaning that everyone opens every file the same way, and every file has the same things in the same place in the same order for the sake of consistency, predictability, and interchangeability. You want to have documented processes, systems, and procedures so you can swap out one associate and throw in another—not completely seamlessly, as there's going to be some transition, but you don't ever want to be held hostage by the attorney or by the secretary who is the only person who knows how to do this job in the firm.

Instead, you want to have documented processes, systems, and procedures so that you can take a reasonably intelligent person off the street, put them through a properly logical and rational onboarding process for a week or two and train them on these documented processes and procedures. And then, you've got objective criteria by which to hold them accountable for the performance of their job.

The result is that you are not only safe from being held hostage by people, but it also helps you with recruiting, training, and managing, and it makes the staff far more profitable. It also makes it easier for the staff to do their jobs because they have clear rules and standards under which to operate as well, which, in turn, leads to less turnover and gets us to the fourth part of a successful law firm.

PART 4: PEOPLE

Do you have a written job description for the job of the receptionist, secretary, paralegal, associate, Rainmaker, etc., that clearly defines what the person in that role is supposed to do? Do you have key performance indicators that you use to engineer each job to be profitable? Do you have objective criteria and clear job descriptions that will give both you and your staff protection? Yes, you need protection from your staff in the event they underperform and imply they were unaware of their duties; and your staff needs protection from you when you come in ranting and raving about why they didn't do this or that.

Job descriptions allow the employee to say, "This is outside the scope of my job. If you want me to put this inside the scope of my job, that's fine. Let's revise my job description." Now, this is not an excuse for someone to just say, "That's not my job." You don't ever want to have someone like that working for you. But you do want people to know clearly whose job is what, because when it's everyone's job, then it becomes no one's job, and things fall through the cracks. Every job needs to be engineered to be profitable for the employee; every job needs to be engineered to be profitable for the clients; and every job needs to be engineered to be profitable for the law firm and for you as the owner.

You also want to have key performance indicators (KPIs) so that you have objective data and metrics by which to judge the performance of your employees. This is how you also can protect yourself from accusations of favoritism when you might have two employees, Bob and Mary let's just say, who each function in the same roles. Except Bob has a big personality, is very friendly, and everyone likes him, whereas Mary keeps her head down and just gets her work done without interacting with you or others in the firm much. You might naturally gravitate more to Mr. Big Personality Bob because he asks about your kids, and you have coffee together from time to time, so Bob gets the bonuses and Mary gets overlooked. However, when you look at clear and objective data, it's obvious that Mary is the more valuable, profitable, and productive employee who is closing cases faster and billing more hours. (More on that later.) Having proper KPIs for each of the job functions in your firm allows you to be objective and consistent in the management of your team.

PART 5: PHYSICAL PLANT

People require things to work with like desks, chairs, pens, computers, and software. Even in the Metaverse, a human being still needs a physical place to work! That's why the fifth part of every successful law firm is the Physical Plant, which may be an office that you rent to provide a place for your staff to work out of, or it may be an office in their home, but your staff needs a place to work. Your clients need a place to meet with you—whether that is in person at your office or via Zoom. Where the work gets done and what resources are utilized to do so is a critical part of your law firm and needs to be congruent with your business plan. Imagine engineering your business plan to produce a growth rate of over 50%, which will call for several new positions/people to be hired to support the firm's growth, but your office is only 1,200 square feet and you're already maxed out on space.

You also have to make sure the physical plant is properly aligned to the business model, which means it has to be properly aligned to the marketing so that you set proper expectations for your prospective new clients when they walk in your doors or hop on a video call. How you are branding yourself in your marketing needs to be mirrored in your physical plant so that your salespeople are selling an honest product and giving people what they came to expect when they were attracted by your marketing.

This is why you need to consider your law firm's physical plant—which includes the documented systems and procedures that run your firm—now and into the future.

PART 6: MONEY & METRICS

The sixth part of every successful law firm is financial controls.

In addition to the typical financial statements (the profit & loss statement, the balance sheet, and the cash flow report) there are other key performance indicators and metrics that you're going to want to keep track of on your dashboard so that you can see at a glance if everything's working properly on any given day. Some reports you may want on your dashboard are:

1. 12-Month Forward-Looking Budget

2. Budget Variance Report

3. Cash Flow Projection (6 weeks)

4. Aged Accounts Receivable Report

5. Cash Position Report (Operating & Trust)

6. WIP (Work in Progress) Report

Think about your car: You probably have a fuel gauge, a temperature gauge, an oil pressure gauge (unless you drive a Tesla), etc. You don't have to *be* a mechanic to know what to do when a red light starts blinking on your dashboard. What you need to know is that when that red light starts blinking, it's time to take the car to a mechanic.

The point of a financial dashboard with all these reports is for you to be able to see that revenues are coming into the firm at the rate your business plan calls for. You should also be able to see that the firm is producing work at a healthy capacity and that the bills and expenses are being paid on time, which tells us the firm's operation is strong.

A very real example of this happened when I was in the jungles of Belize. One day I looked at my dashboard (as I did every day) and I saw a red alert. It wasn't easy, but I found my way to a Wi-Fi connection in a hut in the middle of the jungle. And I got on the phone, and I said, "What's going on with this dashboard?"

I found out that some things that were supposed to be getting done, didn't get done. Thankfully I did not have to leave the jungle, get on a plane, fly back to the office, and fix it. I was able to fix it by remote control, by giving instructions and directions. But the point is, I was able to enjoy my vacation with the confidence of knowing that if there was going to be a problem, I would know about it. More to the point, I've been able to take lots of vacations since, and there is so much peace in knowing that if there's a problem, my dashboard will tell me about it. This truly has changed my life.

That rumble in the jungle happened in 2011. And as much as I work to try and avoid letting things like that happen, I'm actually glad that it *did* happen so early in my business because it showed me that I really could have confidence in my systems. I've taken many vacations for weeks at a time since then with emergency access only. And I can't remember the last time someone called me while I was on vacation with an emergency. But *if* they need me, they know they can reach me. And if there is a problem and my team doesn't feel comfortable reaching out to me, I would be calling *them*. Because I check my dashboard every day. As a word to the wise, a quick look at your dashboard every morning while you're on vacation, makes for a better vacation.

PART 7: YOU

Finally, we get to YOU. Because each of the other parts of your law firm revolve around your financial goals, your personal goals, and your professional goals. The firm is supposed to serve *you,* you are not supposed to live in service to the firm.

Remember, your law firm isn't your baby. It's not going to love you. It's not going to give you a hug. As parents, we would do anything for our children. We live for our children. Sometimes we would *die* for our children. We make all kinds of sacrifices for our children because this is a biological imperative for our species.

But your law firm isn't your baby. You're not supposed to work for your law firm. Your law firm is a business. Your business is supposed to work for *you.*

I've had this conversation with thousands and thousands of lawyers for a few decades now, and I have found that there's a much more practical, professional, ethical, and profitable analogy to use than that of a parent and child when thinking about your relationship with your law firm. The best analogy I've been able to come up with is the farmer and the mule.

Think about why the farmer has a mule: The farmer has a mule so that the mule can pull the farmer's plow. And why does the farmer care about having the plow pulled? So the farmer can grow crops. And why does the farmer care about growing crops? Because the farmer wants to feed the farmer's family. And if the farmer manages the crop rotation efficiently, trains the mule well, and does the job right, there should hopefully be enough crops left over after feeding the farmer's family. See? Profit First. Feed your family first, *then* you can take the crops and share them with everyone else by going to the market and selling them.

Does this mean that you can abuse the mule? No, you cannot.

If you expect the mule to operate at peak performance, can you neglect the mule? No, you can't neglect the mule.

You still have to train, feed, house, care for, and manage the mule if you want the mule to do its job for you and your family. But you ought not be taking pride in how many hours you spend in the barn with the mule.

Everywhere I go, I find lawyers who are bragging about how many hours they spend in the barn with the mule. They're literally bragging about how badly they manage their law firm. They're bragging about how poorly they manage their businesses. They don't call it bragging, of course, they call it commiserating. It's so strange. If you say, "Financially, my law firm's gross revenues have doubled and doubled and doubled again. I've eradicated accounts receivables, my law firm's profits keep growing and growing, and financially I'm doing great. Everything's wonderful." They're all going to say, "You're bragging."

If, on the other hand, you say, "The economy's no good. My accounts receivables are out of control; the clients won't pay!" They're all going to start bragging and competing for whose is worse. "$20,000 in accounts receivables? That's nothing. I've got $30,000 in accounts receivables!"

And then someone else is going to say, "$30,000 in accounts receivables? That's nothing. I've got $40,000!"

They're bragging about their problems.

The problems all start with the owner. The mindset of the owner shows up in the marketing, the sales, the hiring and training and management of staff. It is documented in the processes and the systems and the procedures (or the excuses that they make for trying to avoid creating them).

There are seven main parts of every successful law firm. When I describe this to people, I usually describe it in a linear fashion:

Marketing → Sales → Production → People → Physical Plant → Money & Metrics → You

But in reality, it's more like a wheel with an axle in the middle. Marketing, which leads to sales. Sales, which leads to production. Production, which leads to people. People, which lead to physical plant. Physical plant, which leads to financial controls. And, if you get it all right, those parts produce profits which go back into marketing . . . and round and round the wheel goes.

At the center of it all is *you*.

As soon as you begin taking responsibility for getting and keeping (or getting help to keep) The 7 Main Parts of your law firm in alignment, and then into a process of continual maintenance and improvement . . . that's how quickly you can begin to see your future brighten and your present become less stressful. "About 18 months." That's how long it typically takes to get things turned around.

And it goes by fast when you do it right.

Profit First is a big part of doing things right. To fund all the improvements you're going to want to make once you see what's possible, your law firm must be transformed into a profit-making machine.

We do this in a very small way at first.

So small, you'll hardly even notice it.

In fact, most of the time, there is so much wasted money being spent in a law firm without a proper budget or financial controls that the first round of improved profits will come from wasted money not being wasted anymore.

Just think, your law firm can begin producing more profits for you, which can be reinvested to make your law firm even more profitable, all from wasted money that's most likely "leaking" from your business today. It would be too good to be true, if it wasn't so horrifying to see how many wasted opportunities there are in most small law firms.

■ ■ ■

CHAPTER 6

WHAT IS "PROFIT"?

Here, *we are going to expand our minds* beyond the dictionary's conventional definition of "profit" and "profitable," which only account for financial profits.

Instead, let's think about all the ways a decision or an action can be profitable—that is, where a value is derived in excess of what is given. The value derived might be measured in terms of financial gain, personal gain, and/or professional gain. These tend to be the three main ways we measure profitable activity as entrepreneurs.

Put another way, "profit" is the benefit derived from exchanging anything a person values LESS for something that person values MORE.

So, when I exchange a red marble for a green marble (for example), assuming the exchange was made voluntarily by both parties, then both parties to the transaction must have made a profit, or else they would not have entered and completed the transaction voluntarily. They each must have preferred to have the other marble. Keep in mind, if fraud, force, or trickery was involved, then the transaction was inherently involuntary for at least one of the parties to it, and mutual profit is not assured.

How To Manage A Small Law Firm is FOR profit. We are in favor of people knowingly, intentionally, and voluntarily exchanging things (time, money, opportunities, and even relationships) that they value less to gain time, opportunities, and relationships that they place a higher value on, even if the "thing" being sacrificed for that which is being obtained is highly valued.

In other words, just because I give it up to get something I value more doesn't mean the thing I'm willing to give up has "no" value to me, only that the thing I'm getting is calculated to have even more value to me in either the short term or long term.

For example, if I have a dollar and I also have a problem; you have a need for my dollar and you also have a possible solution or a practiced system or approach that is reasonably calculated to help me solve my problem; and you value the delivery of that solution or service less than you value the dollar; then we can each make a profit by exchanging my dollar for the service you have to offer.

Because even though I value my dollar, I value the opportunity to solve my problem even more; and even though you value the solution you possess or the effort required to provide the service, you value the dollar I have even more.

By way of another very relevant example, I treasure time with my son. But instead of spending time with him right now, I am sitting here writing this book for you. I often knowingly, intentionally, and voluntarily sacrifice time with my son in this way (writing books, attending courses, providing a service, or attending to the management of my business) so I can give him a better life. In this way, I make a "profit." Because as much as I value and enjoy my time with him today, I value my son's future well-being and the feelings I expect to have being able to give him that better future (and avoid the feelings of regret if I can't) even more than the time I give up being with him today. Of course, only your firm's financials are black and white (and hopefully no red). Everything else is a balancing act.

■ ■ ■

Lawyers who do not put Profit First are often at a disadvantage when trying to understand the simple profit-seeking equation that all their clients use when deciding whether to hire a law firm to help them solve their problems.

That's because lawyers who do not put Profit First often fail to derive any financial gain from the transactions and relationships they engage in, and therefore there's often an important element missing from the equation, from their point of view.

Imagine the same scenario described previously where the client has a dollar and a problem that they value the solution for more than the dollar. Here, you have a willing, perhaps even eager, buyer for whom the potential engagement seems pretty simple:

"I have this dollar, which I value LESS than that solution. If I exchange this dollar for that solution, I am at a PROFIT."

But to the lawyer who has no predictable or reliable system to be sure there will be a financial profit at the end of the transaction, the situation appears to be very different:

"I have an opportunity to enjoy time with my family. This stranger has asked me to sacrifice some of the time I'd enjoy with my family to attend to the potential new client's problem, and the potential new client (PNC) has offered to exchange a dollar for that service. But I have no profit-protecting system. And no one on my team is looking out for me to ensure that I'll get to keep any part of that dollar. So, I may wind up sacrificing some precious time with my family to solve the PNC's problem and have no financial profit to show for it."

This simple misalignment explains more problems in the legal industry than I can address in this small book. Correcting this simple misalignment is one of the "secrets" behind the success you'll find inside of hundreds and hundreds of the small law firms my own firm helps manage. Implementing Profit First in your law firm is a meaningful first step you can take today that will help you correct this costly and stressful misalignment between yourself and the clients of your law firm.

Just as How To Manage A Small Law Firm is "for" profit, we are against loss (unprofitable decisions) where loss is by intentional design (knowingly trading something you value more to get something you value less) or the predictable effect of recklessness or lack of clear thinking.

For example, the parent who knows that taking certain actions in their business could help assure a better future for their child but is unwilling to be inconvenienced or go out of their comfort zone today, even though it means a bleaker future for their child and certain regret for the parent themself. This would be an example of an "unprofitable" decision.

Keep in mind, the profitability of the decision can only be judged at the time of the transaction, not after.

So the question is this: Right now, in the present, at the time of the voluntary exchange, with each party as fully informed as reasonably possible, do they both reasonably believe the thing they are getting is worth more to them than whatever is being given (sacrificed)?

If so, it is a profitable exchange.

If not, then it is an unprofitable exchange.

Sadly, people knowingly make unprofitable exchanges all the time because of all sorts of irrational fears, feelings, and untested, unexamined beliefs.

So, when I say How To Manage A Small Law Firm is "for" profit and "against loss," it really means we are for being rational and intentional and thinking things through and doing things for a purpose that is true to yourself.

And when I say I want you to put your profits first, what I really mean is that I want you to put rational thought first.

Want to know more about this? Use this QR code to see a video about an important concept called "**The Doctrine of Sacrifice**" and why How To Manage A Small Law Firm was founded to expose and CRUSH this very dangerous idea that has infected the legal industry.

■ ■ ■

CHAPTER 7

UNDERSTANDING WHY YOUR C.P.A. DOESN'T ABSOLUTELY LOVE PUTTING YOUR PROFITS FIRST

To *begin with, you must understand* that the way you and I see the world as lawyers is very different from the way your C.P.A. has been trained to see the world.

Until you understand just why and how very different these two perspectives are, you will continue to be at an unprofitable disadvantage when hiring and managing the working relationship between your law firm and its C.P.A. and very likely your firm's bookkeeper, too. Because most bookkeepers are trained by C.P.A.s.

Think of this chapter as a "primer." It will probably piss you off. And in the next, I will walk you through something that is at once obvious (once you know where to look) and so bizarre that most people who aren't accountants tend to dismiss the thing as being impossible.

Taken together, these two chapters may rock your world. So, please buckle up because this is going to get rough.

You've heard the question a thousand times: "Do you know a good accountant?" Most law firm owners don't have a business or a finance degree or an M.B.A. or C.P.A. training. And so, they are unaware that as entrepreneurs, we don't need *one* accountant, we need four. Yes, you read that right. To professionally manage the business of your law firm (instead of treating it like a hobby), what you need are FOUR different kinds of accounting services. Just like you don't need just one wheel on your car. To maximize the profitability of your business and minimize the stress in your life, you need all four of these "financial wheels" in your business.

Before you start freaking out about hiring four different professionals to do the job(s) you previously thought just one kind of accountant could do, please stick with me. And keep an open mind. You're going to SAVE money if you do it this way.

But first, let's just get this over with: *Your C.P.A. Took an Oath Against You.* Ouch! I know.

Here's the Oath I took when I was admitted to the Florida Bar in 1998. It's probably pretty similar to the Oath you took as a lawyer, too:

I do solemnly swear: I will support the Constitution of the United States and the Constitution of the State of Florida; I will maintain the respect due to courts of justice and judicial officers; I will not counsel or maintain any suit or proceedings which shall appear to me to be unjust, nor any defense except such as I believe to be honestly debatable under the law of the land; I will employ, for the purpose of maintaining the causes confided in me such means only as are consistent with truth and honor, and will never seek to mislead the judge or jury by any artifice or false statement of fact or law; I will maintain the confidence and preserve inviolate the secrets of my clients, and will accept no compensation in connection with their business except from them or with their knowledge and approval; To opposing parties and their counsel, I pledge fairness, integrity, and civility, not only in court, but also in all written and oral communications; I will abstain from all offensive personality and advance no fact prejudicial to the honor or reputation of a party or witness, unless required by the justice of the cause with which I am charged; I will never reject, from any consideration personal to myself, the cause of the defenseless or oppressed, or delay anyone's cause for lucre or malice. So help me God.

And since I am a member of the Florida Bar (Fla Bar No. 126713), I'm using my State's Bar Rules as an example. But I have worked with law firms across the country and in several other countries, too. And in every state or jurisdiction, there is a rule that is materially similar to this one we have in Florida:

STATE OF FLORIDA'S OATH OF ADMISSION FOR ATTORNEYS[1]

> A lawyer, as a member of the legal profession, is a representative of clients, an officer of the legal system, and a public citizen having special responsibility for the quality of justice.
> As a representative of clients, a lawyer performs various functions.
> As an adviser, a lawyer provides a client with an informed under-standing of the client's legal rights and obligations and explains their practical implications.
> As an advocate, a lawyer zealously asserts the client's position under the rules of the adversary system.
> As a negotiator, a lawyer seeks a result advantageous to the client but consistent with requirements of honest dealing with others.
> As an evaluator, a lawyer acts by examining a client's legal affairs and reporting about them to the client or to others.

No matter to which state Bar you are admitted, I am sure you find Florida's Oath of Attorney and Bar Rules of Professional Conduct to be somewhat familiar and intuitive, yes? You might even say it's "common sense" that a professional advisor owes the client a duty of loyalty, right?

OK, remember when I told you to buckle up? Now hold on tight because we're about to look at the world through the lens of a C.P.A.:[2]

---

1 https://cdn.ymaws.com/www.inbar.org/resource/resmgr/litigation/Oaths.pdf
2 https://pub.aiC.P.A..org/codeofconduct/ethicsresources/et-cod.pdf

**STRUCTURE AND APPLICATION OF THE AICPA CODE
0.300 PRINCIPLES OF PROFESSIONAL CONDUCT**

0.300.030 The Public Interest

.01 The public interest principle. Members should accept the obligation to act in a way that will serve the public interest, honor the public trust, and demonstrate a commitment to professionalism.

.02 A distinguishing mark of a profession is acceptance of its responsibility to the public. The accounting profession's public consists of clients, credit grantors, governments, employers, investors, the business and financial community, and others who rely on the objectivity and integrity of members to maintain the orderly functioning of commerce. This reliance imposes a public interest responsibility on members. The public interest is defined as the collective well-being of the community of people and institutions that the profession serves.

(Excerpts from the AICPA Code of Professional Conduct)

IN OTHER WORDS...

"[Your C.P.A. has sworn an oath to] act in a way that will serve the public interest. [And your C.P.A.'s "public"] consists of [not just YOU but also your] credit grantors, governments, employers, investors, the business and financial community, and others who rely on the objectivity and integrity of [your C.P.A.] to maintain the orderly functioning of commerce. [And so] This reliance imposes a public interest responsibility on [the C.P.A. you are seeking counsel and strategic advice from. And] The public interest is defined as the collective well-being of the community of people and institutions that the profession serves **[NOT JUST YOU!!!]**

> I thought my C.P.A. was my advocate? 😔

> > Nope!

> I thought my C.P.A. was on MY side?

> > Uh, uh. 😊

> I thought my C.P.A. was supposed to be zealous about advancing and protecting MY interests?

> > So did I. Until I learned this the hard way.

> > Did I mention I have a lot of battle scars? 😎

Perhaps this will be easier for you to understand if we stop using the abbreviation "C.P.A." and I spell it out for you.

Your Certified PUBLIC Accountant was trained, took an oath, and practices under a set of rules that require them to protect the PUBLIC against YOU.

"I think you mean my C.P.A. has sworn an oath to protect the public AND me."

No. As you're about to discover in the next chapter, their bible (GAAP) was created to protect the public AGAINST you.

"So, wait a minute RJon, you're telling me that all this time I've been paying my C.P.A. and taking business advice from my C.P.A. and asking my C.P.A. for advice on how to save money on my taxes, etc., etc. . . . you're telling me that this whole time my C.P.A. has been taking my money but looking out for my creditors, the government, and 'the public' instead of only looking out for me?!?!" Yes. That is exactly what I am telling you. And it is 100% completely true. Glad you have that seat belt buckled up now, aren't you?

As officers of the court and fellow brethren, sistren, and personen of the Bar, we abide by certain ethical rules and obligations of truth and candor and civility. But we are also unapologetic advocates for our clients, above all else. We are 100% on the side of our clients against all others. In fact, we are disciplined if we even give the *appearance* of a conflict of interest. We are taught, trained, and swear an oath to be on our clients' side and remain the keepers of our clients' secrets against the world.

As lawyers who own businesses that happen to be law firms, we therefore tend to assume (rather naively, it turns out) that our C.P.A. must be on our side and acts as our advocate, confidante, and advisor. But your Certified PUBLIC Accountant is not on your side. Your Certified PUBLIC Accountant owes a duty to the public, to your investors, to your creditors, and to the government. Your C.P.A. owes a split loyalty to everyone. Including you. But not only you. And in case you didn't know, there is no such thing as an Accountant-Client Privilege.

Take a minute to let it sink in just how radically different our perspective is as lawyers, from the perspective of a C.P.A. Because unless they're also a lawyer, your C.P.A. was not sworn to protect their clients' interests like you and I were. It's like having your defense attorney also working for the other side!

Most C.P.A.s are financial accountants. They are trained to report what has happened in the past in terms of revenue and expenses to protect the government and public interests, first. So, is it any wonder why your C.P.A. and the bookkeepers who get their training from C.P.A.s are more concerned with the "accuracy" of their reporting than they are in helping you develop legal and law-abiding, forward-looking strategies to plan the management of revenues and expenses while advocating (zealously) for the maximization of profits you take from your business?!?!

"So why do I need a C.P.A. at all?"

The truth of the matter is that unless you are operating a publicly traded company, you don't. What you need is a professional tax preparer who may or may not also be a C.P.A. In the interest of full disclosure, my professional tax preparer is also a C.P.A., and all things being equal, I believe you ought to have a C.P.A. preparing your taxes for you, too. Just don't ask them to help you plan how you're going to grow your business or keep more of your profits.

Which brings us to . . .

Management Accounting versus Financial Accounting.

Financial Accountants are not the same thing as Management Accountants. Management Accountants are sometime C.P.A.s who have taken additional training. But not every Management Accountant is a C.P.A., and very few C.P.A.s are also Management Accountants. Think of it this way: Your Management Accountant sits in the front seat next to you with a road map, helping you plan ahead, suggesting alternative routes, warning you of upcoming traffic conditions and road hazards, and recommending, suggesting, and strategizing to proactively help you maximize your profits.

Your Financial Accountant was trained to sit in the back seat and look out the back window to see where you've been. They're trained to keep an accurate and correct log that "accounts for" where you've been, what you've done, and what has already happened. Your Financial Accountant is a historian. Your Management Accountant is your copilot.

"Your Financial Accountant is a historian. Your Management Accountant is your copilot."

We build C.F.O.s and bookkeepers who do not suck, out of Management Accountants, not Financial Accountants.

And the teams we deploy across the country to run our Tax Strategy Workshops are staffed by Management Accountants, not just C.P.A.s.[3]

So now you know why your C.P.A. and perhaps your bookkeeper, too (who was probably trained by a Financial Accountant), cried "Blasphemy!" when you shared Profit First with them. In the next chapter it's going to get really ugly when I dismantle their bible for you and show you why GAAP wasn't meant for you. But first we have to finish rubbing some salt in the wound I may have just caused in your relationship with your Certified PUBLIC Accountant and the bookkeepers they train to protect the public against you. It might be a good idea now to take a few deep breaths before you proceed.

As If All That Wasn't Bad Enough . . .

Just as YOU probably didn't take even a single class in your life about the business of how to manage a small law firm . . . guess who likely never took even a single class in their life, either, about the business of how to manage an accounting firm (or a law firm)? That's right! Your accountant!

Accountants are trained to be technicians. They're trained to account for where all the revenue came from. They're trained to account for where all the revenue went to when it became an "expense." And if there happens to be anything left over, they're trained to call that "profit" and give it to you.

Your accountant may be very good at accurately accounting for where your firm's revenues are coming from and going to, but they're not necessarily very entrepreneurial. They're not Business Growth Advisors. And if you dig into it a little bit, there's a very good chance you will find that they can't even grow their own business.

---

3 . . . did I mention we also run a series of amazing "triple your money back guaranteed" **Tax Strategy Workshops**, to help law firm owners keep more of the profits we help you make?

Want to Put This to the Test?

Ask your C.P.A. or your bookkeeper if you can please see a copy of their written business plan. Ask what metrics they are using to track the performance of their own marketing strategy. Ask if they even have a marketing strategy that extends beyond when next month's rent is due. Do they have any sort of sales system to convert prospects into paying clients while they're away from the office with defined "Emergency Access Only" for weeks or months at a time?

Ask the C.P.A. or bookkeeper whose advice you rely upon to share with you some of their own written job descriptions they use to hire, train, or manage their own staff. What sort of ongoing internal training programs do they have in place? What are the key performance indicators they use to measure the performance of their staff fairly and objectively?

Say to them: "I really want to improve the profitability of my business. Would you please share with me how you document your own most important workflow processes and procedures and how you systematize the workflow in your firm?"

And if you really want to see the bloom fall off the rose, ask your C.P.A. or your bookkeeper what financial reports they review for their own business, how often, and why.

I believe these are all very reasonable questions for a client to ask their trusted tax, financial, and business management advisors to help evaluate how much stock you'll put in their advice. Don't settle for less.

Okay, so now you know that to professionally manage the business of your law firm:

1. You'll need a Financial Accountant to prepare your taxes, issue reports to your lenders and shareholders, etc.

2. You'll need a bookkeeper to gather, collect, keep track of, and prepare key financial reports that you can learn to use to understand

and anticipate what is really going on "under the hood" in your business.[4]

3. You'll want to have a Management Accountant to help you plan, strategize, interpret, evaluate, and make strategic plans for your future, based on the financial reports your bookkeeper will prepare.[5]

4. And if you are going to be really smart about maximizing the profitability of your business, you should also have a dedicated Tax Strategist advising you at least 12 months in advance at all times.

"But this seems too expensive!"

No, I'm not in your head. I've just had this conversation with thousands of law firm owners to know what you may be thinking right now. So please, allow me to share with you this practical example to put your mind at ease.

Let's assume your fast-growing law firm grossed $500,000 last year. It operated at a 25% Total Owner Benefit "profit" margin. Your own personal "blended" federal tax rate is 30%. For the purposes of this example, we're going to assume you live in a place with no state or city taxes.

Here's the math: $500,000 x 25% = $125,000 x 70% (the part you get to keep after paying 30% in taxes) = $87,500/year.

---

4 **Two excellent resources** include:
   Crabtree, G. (2011). *Simple Numbers, Straight Talk, Big Profits! 4 Keys to Unlock Your Business Potential.*
   Tracy, T. (2020). *How to Read a Financial Report: Wringing Vital Signs Out of the Numbers.* 9th Edition.
5 Either your Management Accountant or your Financial Accountant may be the one to supervise your bookkeeper. But if it was up to me I'd want your bookkeeper supervised by a Management Accountant.

To get an extra $10,000 in after-tax disposable income to spend on your child's tuition, toys, or braces, you'd need your firm to gross an extra $57,000.

($57,000 x .25) x .70 = $10,000

So, would you rather do all the marketing, sales, legal work, and supervision of staff required to gross an extra $57,000 . . . or would you prefer to work with a good bookkeeper and a proper tax strategist to save $10,000 on your taxes out of the same $500,000?

And while we're on this subject, let me ask you another relevant question: Would you rather do all the marketing, sales, management, and legal work required to collect $500,000, see how much of it gets allocated by your firm's bookkeeper and C.P.A. as expenses, and you get to keep whatever is left over . . . or would you rather work with a Profit First Professional who will protect your profits first, then help you figure out how to make your business work with what's left over?

Yes, this may require you to learn some new, better, and more profitable ways of running your business. But what if it didn't have to require you to work more hours, and this approach put more financial profits directly into your pocket—and made your clients and your staff happier, too?

"But won't this all cost me more money? Isn't this going to be more expensive? I still don't get it!"

Yes and no.

The word "expense" is synonymous with the word "cost." They both mean the price you pay. These words are both nouns. The word "expensive" is an adjective. Nouns identify a thing. Adjectives modify nouns.

If you put a price tag of $100 on a bottle of water, that is a noun. This is simply the price or cost being charged for the bottle of water. It does not describe the value of the water.

Paying $100 for a bottle of water in the middle of a clean freshwater lake might seem too high a price to pay, relatively speaking. One might say, "That's an expensive bottle of water." But if I offer to bring you that same bottle of drinkable water to a remote location in the middle of the desert with no other source of freshwater available, then the $100 expense (compared to the value of your life) suddenly isn't very "expensive" at all.

Yes, it is true that the price you will pay for a **Profit First Certified Professional** will tend to be higher than the cost of a bookkeeper or an accountant who will not help you protect your profits. Profit First Certified Professionals do tend to cost more. But they're far less expensive.

Okay, now I really want you to take a few deep breaths because we're about to dismantle GAAP. Don't worry, there's no math involved. Just common sense.

*Want to learn much, much more about **how to evaluate the quality and relevance of the financial reports** you're getting from your bookkeeper or accountant? Hint: "Accurate" is strictly for amateurs.*

· · ·

CHAPTER 8

WHY GENERALLY ACCEPTED ACCOUNTING PRINCIPLES (GAAP) ARE NOT MEANT FOR YOU

From the last chapter, you should now have a fuller understanding of why and how you, as the owner of a law firm, tend to see the world from such a very different perspective than your Certified Public Accountant and very likely the bookkeepers who you've worked with because they were probably trained by C.P.A.s.

C.P.A.s, and the bookkeepers they train, worship their Generally Accepted Accounting Principles (GAAP) as if they are gospel. And I want you to feel liberated when you recognize that GAAP isn't gospel. I want you to feel empowered by the knowledge that GAAP is not the only way to manage a small law firm to profitability. I want you to feel encouraged knowing that GAAP is certainly not the best way and has never been the best way to manage your law firm to maximum profitability. I want you to clearly understand that GAAP wasn't meant for you and me and that it's a mismatch. So, if your ego or self-esteem has been taking a beating—"I know I'm a good lawyer and I work so hard, so why can't I take any profits from my law firm?"—I am hoping these statements above give you some relief and the courage to lay down the law to your bookkeeper and accountant that you are going to liberate yourself from

61

GAAP and begin taking advantage of Profit First Accounting Principles (PFAP), instead.

> # WARNING:
> You're about to learn more about GAAP's history and origins than many of those who preach it as gospel have ever imagined. Keep this chapter in mind the next time your Certified PUBLIC Accountant or bookkeeper tells you to leave your profit until last because of their precious GAAP.

Let's go back in time . . .

Imagine it's the 1920s—I'm talking about the prohibition era, the Harlem Renaissance, flapper girls, jazz . . . everything that made that era an amazing time, until, of course, it was no longer amazing or very prosperous.

Back then, people were buying stocks on margin and making buckets of money. Buying stocks on margin meant people were basically buying stocks on credit. So, if someone had $1,000 in life savings (remember, this is the 1920s) and invested their life savings to acquire $10,000 worth of stock because they could get it with 10% down on margin, then their entire life could change for the better practically overnight if the stock price were to increase by just a little bit. For example, if the stock went from $10,000 to $11,000, the investor's life savings would have just doubled. And for many people, that's exactly what happened. Imagine doubling your life savings overnight, just like that!

If the investor's stock pick went to $20,000, they could make a $9,000 profit on an investment of just $1,000. That's a 900% gain. Multiply your life savings by 90 to understand what a huge incentive people had during those times to invest their life savings into the stock market on margin.

But is it really an "investment" if you can't tell anything about the financial health of the company? What if: Company "A" issues financial reports one way; Company "B" issues financial reports a different way; and Company "C" issues its financial reports differently, too!

How do you imagine the average investor was supposed to make an apples-to-apples comparison between three different companies or manage their investments when so many of the publicly traded companies each kept their books in completely different ways?

The question above is obviously a rhetorical question because clearly, the answer is that they couldn't!

And now, think of what an impossible challenge it would have been for regulators to regulate thousands of those different companies when they were each presenting their financials, perhaps accurately, but using different standards.

Then on October 24th, 1929, there was a panic and stocks lost about 11% of their value. Those who had bought all their stocks on margin and didn't have additional resources to cover the margin call were wiped out. The following Monday, October 28th, 1929, also known as Black Monday, the stock market went down another 12%, and most of those who were able to survive the first drop were wiped out by the second one due to the lack of capital reserves or lack of confidence enough to put more of their capital at risk. And then, on Black Tuesday, October 29th, 1929, the stock market dropped another 11% and practically everyone was wiped out.

People think the 1929 stock market crash was caused by widespread fraud. It wasn't. It was caused by widespread over-speculation because investors didn't have enough reserve capital to respond to a margin call. And then, there was panic because investors were over-leveraged but didn't have reliable information about the true financial health of the companies they'd invested in due to the lack of any uniform standards for the presentation of financials. And yes, there was also a lot of fraudulent activity, or at least activity that would be deemed to be fraudulent under today's rules and regulations for how publicly traded companies are to keep their books and report financial activities.

"Something Must Be Done!"

Indeed, something *was* done. First, the American Institute of Accountants (AIA), which later became the American Institute of Certified Public Accountants (AICPA), organized a special committee to recommend five "broad principles of accounting that have won fairly general acceptance."

It is important for you to be aware of something the committee acknowledged when it made its recommendations. The committee noted that:

> *"Within quite wide limits, it is relatively unimportant to the investor what precise rules or conventions are adopted by a corporation in reporting its earnings if he knows what method is being followed and is assured that it is followed consistently from year to year."*

In other words, the committee acknowledged it doesn't much matter which approach we agree on, so long as it's transparent and consistent. What they were going for was transparency and consistency. Keep this in mind because it will help you connect the dots a couple pages from now and ultimately keep more of the profits your law firm is capable of generating!

In 1933, The Securities Act of 1933 was created and passed into law. This legislation had two main goals: to ensure more transparency in financial statements so investors could make informed decisions about investments, and to establish laws against misrepresentation and fraudulent activities in the securities markets.[6]

---

6 http://archives.C.P.A.journal.com/2005/105/infocus/p18.htm

There's that word again, "transparency."

Then, in 1936, the AIA organized a committee to agree on a standard set of accounting principles. The committee was composed of 18 practitioners and three accounting academics, all serving on a part-time basis, with a small research staff. The Institute published its *Examinations of Financial Statements* later that year, which is where the term "generally accepted accounting principles" (GAAP) was first introduced.

In 1938, the SEC adopted GAAP as "the" standard.

Did you notice the three common themes that kept popping up?

- Transparency

- Consistency

- Accuracy (not misrepresentative of facts)

Did you notice what was not mentioned?

Nowhere did anyone involved in the creation of GAAP ever claim it was the only way to transparently, consistently, and accurately report the financial conditions of a company. No one from the committee ever even claimed GAAP was necessarily the best way. No one involved in the promulgation of GAAP was trying to find a way to maximize or protect the companies' profitability. It was all about transparency, consistency, and accuracy.

And when is the last time you ever saw a committee of 18 people produce "the best" of anything?

Committees are where the best ideas usually go to die and compromises are made, instead. The original version of GAAP was the product of negotiations, arguments, and compromises. The goal of the committee was to standardize financial reporting to make it easier for investors in publicly traded companies to make apples-to-apples comparisons and to make it easier for regulators to do their job.

Oh, and guess what else?

Almost every single year since its creation, there have been some—sometimes major—amendments, adjustments, ongoing debates, and changes made to GAAP.[7] So, not only was GAAP hastily created as an unapologetic compromise, meant to facilitate easier regulation of publicly traded companies, but it keeps changing too!

That is what your C.P.A. and your bookkeeper keep using as their excuse to put your profits LAST instead of first in their order of priority for the financial management of your NON-PUBLICLY TRADED law firm.

And just so you don't gloss over the importance of what I've just said, I'm going to repeat that last part again: Your Law Firm Is NOT a Publicly Traded Company.

So, you are not REQUIRED to manage your law firm in strict or even in loose compliance with GAAP if you don't want to. And you shouldn't. Because GAAP puts your profits last. Doesn't it make so much more sense to put your profits first, instead?

If you're thinking to yourself that you're not a securities lawyer (or maybe you are), that you didn't pick up this book to learn how to invest in the stock market, and that your law firm isn't a publicly traded company, I'm going to repeat this for the third time: YOUR LAW FIRM IS NOT A PUBLICLY TRADED COMPANY!

So, by now, maybe you're thinking to yourself: "This has nothing to do with me!"

YES! You are correct. GAAP has nothing to do with you. THAT'S MY WHOLE POINT!

GAAP has nothing to do with you.

---

7 http://archives.C.P.A.journal.com/2005/105/infocus/p18.htm

Generally Accepted Accounting Principles were created by a committee that was formed following the Securities Act of 1933. The committee was charged with the responsibility to come up with a set of accounting principles that the whole committee could "generally" agree on. More importantly, GAAP was created for the convenience of regulators who needed to have standards to regulate the entire financial market following the stock market crashes of 1929. How else were they going to regulate the reporting requirements of thousands of different companies? Regulators needed a way to standardize the reporting requirements, make comparisons, and monitor compliance by thousands of different companies, operating in a wide range of different industries. And while it is generally a good thing to establish a standard within financial markets, what does that have to do with the business of running a small law firm that doesn't issue securities to anyone? The correct answer is NOTHING!

Yet your accountant and likely your bookkeepers are trained to get and keep your law firm in compliance with GAAP. This means that while the methods being used to manage the finances and produce profits in your law firm may be accurate and generally accepted, they could be so much more.

Yes, I know I am repeating myself a lot in this chapter. BUT THAT IS ONLY BECAUSE IT IS YOUR FINANCIAL LIFE WE ARE TALKING ABOUT.

So no, I don't mind repeating myself and printing a few extra pages IF IT SAVES YOUR FAMILY'S FINANCIAL FUTURE!

GAAP, which has been in a constant state of flux since the term was first coined in the 1930s, was created so that there was a *generally accepted* way of presenting a set of financials. This doesn't mean it's the best way to report a set of financials, and it certainly doesn't mean it's the only way to cast a set of financials. It simply means that GAAP was the only way that the 18 accountants, who got together back in the 1930s to regulate the financial markets, could all agree upon.

Essentially, the standards set by GAAP consist of the best way to present a set of financials that all 18 accountants could agree on and that no one fought too much over. Because that's what committees do! And since (regrettably) we live in a world full of people who are more concerned with not rocking the boat than living up to their full potential, we now end up with most Certified PUBLIC Accountants and bookkeepers who accept GAAP as if it is a force of nature, which it isn't!

Although you may be a bold and independent thinker when it comes to the practice of law and in other areas of your life, there's a very good chance that you've been thinking a lot like a lemming when it comes to the profitability of your law firm.

To be fair, I never even thought twice about why I was "supposed" to keep track of my financials using GAAP, until I began suffering the ill effects of it and had to rethink:

- "Why am I accounting for my profit last?"

- "Why am I allowing a bookkeeper or an accountant to dictate to me how much profit I'll enjoy from my business?"

- "Whose rules am I following? Do they even make sense for me? Why am I doing it this way? What's the best thing that could happen if I did things differently? What's the worst thing that could happen?"[8]

Revenues minus expenses equals profit—that's GAAP. That is what is "generally accepted." But it doesn't have to be that way. And it's not necessarily the best way to do it. GAAP is simply what is generally accepted.

---

8 It turns out the best thing is now into the multiple 8 figures and the worst thing was a few heated discussions with some accountants and bookkeepers.

And while GAAP may be an accurate way to account for these three important categories in a business (revenues, expenses, and profit), it is not the only way to account for the relationship between these three categories. In fact, the decision to account for revenue, expenses, and profit in accordance with GAAP creates some unintended and quite undesirable side effects in a law firm. Chief amongst these undesirable side effects is that it puts the most important part of your business—profit—LAST! Almost as if it should be an afterthought.

GAAP also tends to disempower owners of law firms because it treats profit as a side effect. As if it's a matter of luck or chance whether or not your law firm will be profitable. It is so much better in so many ways when you treat profit as a program instead of a matter of chance. As a lawyer, you would never leave things to luck or chance for your clients. Don't keep tolerating it when your bookkeeper or accountant leaves the profitability of your law firm to luck or chance for you!

GAAP also messes with your mindset because it explicitly encourages the notion that we as entrepreneurs should work for our businesses instead of our businesses working for us. Think about the premise behind GAAP:

GAAP: REVENUES – EXPENSES = PROFIT

This formula reflects the following notion:

1. You're going to work however hard you must work to get your law firm to generate revenue, and then

2. You're going to let everyone else, including vendors, professional service providers, and employees, line up and take as much of the revenue as they want, and then

3. You and your family will find a way to survive on whatever is
    left over.

That's an unhealthy relationship to have between you and your business. It creates an environment and a mindset that breeds all kinds of poor business decisions that ultimately hurt your clients and your staff. Oh, and also your family.

But there is obviously a better way, or I wouldn't be writing this book, *Profit First For Lawyers*, and Mike wouldn't have written the original *Profit First* book, which again, I highly recommend you read or listen to.

∎ ∎ ∎

Now, if you're anything like me, then you probably went through school like a crammer. If I got an assignment at the beginning of the semester, it didn't matter if I had the whole semester to work on it; I would be in the library during the last week of the semester, cramming to finish the assignment. So yes, it took me an entire semester to get the paper done. But if the professor had given me a month, I'd have gotten it done in a month. If I'd been given a week, I'd have found a way to get it done in a week.

Similarly, when you put profits first, you force creativity, ingenuity, and innovation into your business. This is a healthy thing for a business. And it's good for your staff and your law firm's clients, too! Forcing yourself to find ways to make your business work with what's left over after you have taken the profits out of the firm and protected those profits for your family outside of the business is also good for your family. Really good!

When we implement Profit First Accounting Principles in your law firm, we begin by deciding ahead of time what percentage of every dollar of revenue we are going to scoop off the top and protect for you and your family. Then, we get busy getting creative and finding ways to make the business meet your high standards of performance with what's left over.

This leverages the most valuable asset you have in your business: your creativity. And it works beautifully over and over again every time we implement it with the more than 600 small law firms we help manage.

Is everyone always happy? No.

Because all of a sudden, your law firm's marketing vendors are being held accountable for objectively measured ROI. All of a sudden, your staff has rational and fair (to you) key performance indicators that their performance is being objectively measured by. All of a sudden, decisions are being made against a criterion that puts your best interests first instead of last. You start using facts and not just feelings (or ego).

One of the biggest benefits of Profit First is that when you take the profits out first, you force the business to live on what's left over, and suddenly, it gets to (is "forced to") benefit from your creative brilliance as an entrepreneur to spark ingenuity and efficiency in your organization. This is a healthy thing for your law firm. And it's not only professionally gratifying for you as the owner, but it's more financially profitable, too!

Now, I'm not saying that you might not ever have to present a set of financials in accordance with GAAP to appease your lender. Much like you would put on your Sunday best, you give them the financials the way they want to see them, of course.

But for your regular month-to-month operations, GAAP is not relevant. In fact, it's not helpful, and it's not conducive to having a profitable law firm.

I know, I've been going on and on about this. It's only because I care. So, I'll just say these final words on this point and hope that I've said enough to empower you to stand up and advocate for yourself the next time your accountant and bookkeeper preach that GAAP is gospel.

GAAP sucks.

■ ■ ■

CHAPTER 9

TOTAL OWNER
BENEFITS (TOB)

> ## "How *PROFITABLE* Is Your Law Firm"?
> ## (Compared To Mine)

To *protect your sanity*, I'd encourage you to be prepared with an answer to this question: "How Profitable Is This Law Firm?" And ask yourself the question every day before someone else does. Keep in mind, however, that depending on who is asking, the question could have a very different meaning.

For example, when another lawyer asks, "How profitable is your law firm?" they often mean: "compared to mine." Or they could mean, "Should I buy it?" or "Would you consider coming to work for me?"

When a prospective lender is asking, "How profitable is your law firm?" they probably want to know if you'll be a good customer who will borrow lots of money and pay it back on time.

And when your spouse or significant other asks, "How profitable is this law firm?" they're probably looking for some reassurances that all the sacrifices you and your family have made will be worth it.

But the most important opinion about the profitability of your law firm that you must be concerned with is your own. And here's where it gets tricky because as the owner of the business, we must (should) take more into consideration than what is conventionally understood to be "profit." As entrepreneurs who built our firms from nothing and who wake up every day to do it again, we must ask ourselves a deeper question: "Compared to what?"

For example, let's say you and I had the opportunity to invest in two different firms.

FIRM "A"

This law firm will give you $1 million of personal income. Firm "A" will require you to work 70 hours a week, doing work you hate for clients you despise. And you never get to take a vacation or else the wheels will fall off because there are no documented policies, procedures, or operating systems that empower the staff to keep the machine running while you are away. But you will personally earn $1 million.

FIRM "B"

Firm "B" will give you $500,000 of personal income. This law firm requires you to work an average of 50 hours a week, doing work you find meaningful for clients you care about. Firm "B" has been equipped with good enough operating systems and staff to allow you time off for all the federal holidays. Plus, you can take a REAL vacation for 30 consecutive days each year with "Emergency Access Only" and a high degree of confidence that while you are away, each of the 7 Main Parts of the law firm will keep going and even growing in your absence. This way, you can actually enjoy your vacation with the confidence that when you get back, you won't find a smoldering pile of $#!+ waiting for you. But you will personally earn half as much from Firm "B" as compared to what you will personally earn from Firm "A".

- Which firm do you think your banker, your C.P.A., and your bookkeeper would tell you is more "profitable"?

- Which firm do you think your spouse or significant other would say is more profitable?

- Which law firm do you imagine most of the lawyers you hang around with would consider to be the more profitable firm?

- Most important, which firm would most contribute to YOUR happiness?

Admittedly, these are extreme examples, but which of these two firms would you prefer to invest your time, energy, and attention to grow?

No, my friend, "happiness" isn't accounted for in Generally Accepted Accounting Principles. Neither is peace of mind, propensity for burnout, or the quality of your life. Remember, your law firm is supposed to work for you. It's supposed to serve you professionally, personally, and financially, not "just" financially. You may have a very hard time ever understanding just why and how differently your C.P.A. and your banker see your law firm versus the relationship you have with your firm until you understand this important point: Your business is supposed to work for YOU.

For years, I used to conduct VIP Days from my boat. We'd normally take three firms at a time. Once per quarter, the owners of three different law firms, each with a "plus one," would travel from across the country to have this unique business growth experience.

At one time, these became so popular that groups of highly entrepreneurial law firm owners got together and formed "Boat Groups." And for several years, we had standing appointments once per quarter with the same groups of amazingly fast-growing law firm owners. It was fun and financially profitable—enough to pay for the boat and all its related operating costs with enough left over to buy the dock. It was a wonderful time of my life and career.

Captain Glenn would take care of all the details, and we'd go *Out ON The Office* for an entrepreneurially mind-expanding day. We'd go snorkeling, scuba diving, fishing, or just exploring. And sometimes we got rained out, and we'd scramble to find something else to do. Once, we took the sprinter van in the pouring-down rain to an art museum to experience a fully immersive room that was created where you'd just sit there and feel like you were in Monet's turn-of-the-century Paris.

Some of the greatest inspirations and most "out of the box" ideas that still drive the growth of How To Manage A Small Law Firm, even past $30 million dollars as I write this, came to me during those "Boat Days." But my bankers and my C.P.A. hated it when I took a whole day to take these small groups of entrepreneurs *Out On The Office*. Because the financial profit from those Boat Days paled in comparison to what we earned every time I stepped onto a stage, hosted a webinar, or invested a day "in" the office with my Leadership Team.

But recall my definition of a "Successful" business. To be worthy of being called a "Successful" business, your firm must serve you financially, it must serve you personally, and it must *also* serve you professionally. Two out of three may be enough to win a game of paper, rock, scissors; but neither your business, your personal life, or your career is a game, so two out of three isn't enough. It's certainly not enough to sustain the kind of growth we've had over so many years. The "secret" to building the sort of fast growth, high profits, and fun-to-run firm How To Manage A Small Law Firm is famous for building, is to build a business that gives you all three. So no, those "Boat Days" didn't maximize the financial profits of our firm. But they produced professional and personal profits for me like you'd have to experience yourself to believe. Presumably, those Boat Days produced enough profits for all the entrepreneurs, too, who came back again and again until I discontinued the program.

Let me share with you something that neither your banker, your C.P.A., or any of those conventionally unhappy law firm owners you'll meet at any bar function will tell you.

There's just no way for GAAP to "account for" the profits that come from hearing the ripples of water making way for the bows of your boat as your captain idles out the channel with a gentle bay breeze blowing. Nor is GAAP set up to account for the value of the energy you get as a creative entrepreneur from listening to the nervous and excited chatter of conversations all around you between other highly successful entrepreneurs who are each already beginning to feel their mindset shift as the possibilities for a day of exponential growth begin to unfold before them.

Your banker wants to be sure your firm can honor the terms of its loan and clear its line of credit for 30 days each year as a way to test the financial viability of the business. Your Certified PUBLIC Accountant wants to correctly and accurately account for what has already happened in the past. Most of your professional colleagues may just be trying to survive.

They'll all marvel when, over more than a dozen years, your business "somehow manages" to grow and keep growing by more than TEN THOUSAND PERCENT.[9] They'll write it off as "luck." Some may even try to explain it away in other ways. Because a big part of what causes the business of a professional services firm to grow isn't accounted for in GAAP; it's invisible and therefore deemed irrelevant by those who can't hear the music; and so, they say we are crazy, those of us who are dancing.

---

9 In 2021, the last full year before this book was written, my firm grossed $22 million dollars. In 2010 this firm grossed $200,000. (($2MM- $200K)/$200K) x 100 = 10,900% growth. FYI 10X refers to 100% growth. This is more like 100X ☺

It can be a very lonely place to be the owner of a highly successful professional services firm because it requires the courage and strength of conviction to turn your back on "conventional wisdom." This is why I asked you at the beginning of this chapter to be prepared with your own definition of what it means TO YOU for a law firm to be "successful." Be sure to stop and take a moment from time to time to let it all sink in and quietly thank the person you used to be who had the courage to turn their back on convention by taking the road less traveled, which leads to uncommon results. The person who had the courage, and who cared enough about the future you to make all those sacrifices. And who likely suffered all those slings and arrows from all the disapproving critics of your being so "unconventional." GAAP has no way to account for the satisfaction of knowing that it was all "worth it." There is no place on the balance sheet for the freedom to live life on your terms.

So, before we get to the "real" point of this chapter, I just want to encourage you to take a moment now, away from your bookkeeper or accountant and anyone else who thinks that the only way to measure the profitability of your business is on a balance sheet . . . and consider how else you are going to measure how profitable your business is for you.

Okay, after about my first decade of working exclusively with law firm owners to make their firms work for them (instead of them working for their law firm) and helping thousands and thousands and thousands of law firm owners to make their businesses wildly profitable in all the ways that really matter (including financially) back in about 2009, I finally figured out how to help our Members answer the question that so many law firm owners love to ask each other:

"How Profitable Is Your Law Firm?"
(Compared to Mine)

I finally figured out that the only rational way to respond to this question is to ask for clarification:

"I'll be happy to answer your question about
how profitable my law firm is. But first, please
clarify what you mean by 'profit.'"

This isn't a "strategy" or a clever "tactic."
It's a legitimate question.
And if the person asking you how profitable your law firm is can't tell you what they mean by "profit" or "profitable," then you should know going into that conversation that you're probably wasting your time.

"It depends on what you mean by 'profit.'"

This answer will set you free. And as a result, this way of thinking will make your law firm far more profitable, too.
Now, before we begin, I want to acknowledge that the first part of this book has probably been pretty easy for you because it hasn't involved

any math. But the math that follows will be simple, I promise. So please, don't skip over what comes next because it will set you free!

And please, don't tell yourself that this doesn't apply to your law firm because of your practice area; because your firm works on a contingency fee basis; or because you practice law in South Dakota where, according to one lawyer I met while out on The National CLE Tour,[10] apparently I don't know what I'm talking about "because bookkeeping just doesn't work like that out here."[11]

If you're feeling uncomfortable with the math, please go here to watch a video in which I'll walk you through it — nice and easy.

"How *PROFITABLE* Is Your Law Firm"?
(Compared To Mine)

To answer this question, let's compare the Profit and Loss (P&L) Statements of your law firm to the P&Ls of two other typical law firm owners you can expect to meet at any bar function. They'll be Lawyer Y

---

10 www.NationalCLETour.com

11 Yes, fear really does cause some otherwise very smart lawyers to say some surprisingly moronic things. To themselves, and others.

and Lawyer Z—you are Lawyer X in this example. You all three correctly agree that each of your respective firms has collected gross revenues of $500,000 in the past 12 months. And all three of you manage your firms and report taxes on a cash basis.[12]

Okay, so you all three get together. There are probably beverages involved. And you compare (ahem) "notes" as follows:

- You report honestly and accurately that your P&L shows a 10% profit;

- Lawyer Y reports honestly and accurately that her law firm's P&L shows a 15% profit; and

- Lawyer Z reports, with no small degree of pride, that his firm made a 20% profit.

As Lawyer Z says this, you can't help but notice the not-so-subtle insinuation that he thinks his law firm's profit margin is clear evidence that he is a better lawyer (and possibly a better human being) than the both of you.

And now, based on the belief that Lawyer Z has a law firm that is generating a 20% profit—compared to Lawyer Y's own measly 15% profit and your law firm's embarrassingly low 10% profit—Lawyer Y begins to fall into line and starts soliciting and taking bad law firm management advice from Lawyer Z, who doesn't mind the attention. Fortunately, you've read this book, so you know better. Because, as we are about to see, while it's true that all three law firms grossed the same amount, yours is

---

12 Our Canadian friends are required to keep their books on an accrual basis, not on a cash basis. The principles of this example translate very easily to books kept on an accrual basis. For purposes of this example we're going to use cash basis because it's easier for most lawyers who didn't study accounting or bookkeeping, to understand.

giving you more Total Owner Benefits than Y's gives her and more than Lawyer Z's law firm gives him—even though yours is the least "profitable," according to all the accountants.

So, let's get into this and help you see why Total Owner Benefits really will make your law firm more profitable, and why limiting your thinking to the conventional definition of "profit" will make you crazy.

We use "Total Owner Benefits" as a tool to compare real profits that a law firm delivers in service to the owners as opposed to only the financial profits the law firm can return to investors, which is the only thing GAAP concerns itself with.

There are three components to Total Owner Benefits:

1. **The salary the firm pays you.** This shows up on your W-2 form that your tax preparer uses to report the earned income you get from doing work for the firm. In other words, this is what you get paid for the labor you provide to the firm in your role as an employee of the firm. Ideally, the firm should only pay you what it would cost the firm to pay anyone else other than you to do the same job(s) you do in your role as an employee of the firm.

2. **The technical profits you take from the business as its owner.** This is reflected on schedule K-1, IRS Form 1065. You don't pay Social Security or Medicare taxes on this unearned income. Regardless of whether you take our advice and take your profits first or last, taxable profits are still the difference between revenues and expenses.

3. **Owner benefits.** These are the expenses that your tax strategist should be helping you think through and strategize around

at the beginning of the year so that the firm can incur these expenses instead of you personally paying for them with your own after-tax-dollars. Your law firm is a business. And as such, its expenses can be arranged to legitimately incur many expenses and provide you, as the owner, with some unique and valuable benefits.

Again, this is one of the many ways that a management accountant is very different from a financial accountant or a mere tax preparer.

Recall from chapter 7 that your C.P.A. doesn't really work for you and that your financial accountant took an oath to protect the public against you. Therefore, if your tax preparer only has C.P.A. training, then chances are they are probably not calling you in the last quarter of every year to schedule an appointment to proactively (and very profitably) plan out your tax strategy for next year. And your tax preparer probably is not charging you enough to check in with you every quarter to then adjust the plan to maximize your tax savings. So, the next time your financial accountant or tax preparer gives you a bill, before you thank them for saving you a few pennies on their fee, I want you to stop and consider how much happier you might be if they charged you twice as much and saved you ten times as much on your taxes.

So, back to our three law firm owners: Lawyer Z with his impressive 20% profit margin, Lawyer Y, who is still impressed with Lawyer Z because her GAAP-compliant financial statement shows only 15% profit, and you with your paltry 10% profit margin that the other two make fun of because obviously if you were a better lawyer, your law firm would be more profitable. And remember, all three of your firms earned and collected the exact same amount. Now consider this:

Example 1:

	Lawyer X ($500k gross revenue)	Lawyer Y ($500k gross revenue)	Lawyer Z ($500k gross revenue)
W-2 Earned Income	$50,000	$40,000	$0
K-1 Income	$50,000 (10% PROFIT)	$75,000 (15% PROFIT)	$100,000 (20% PROFIT)
Owner Benefits	$50,000	$10,000	$0
Total Owner Benefits	$150,000	$125,000	$100,000

Notice that each of these firms earned the same $500,000 of gross revenue by providing valuable solutions to improve the lives and businesses of their clients.

Lawyer Z: "Mr. Braggadocio's" law firm provided him with a grand total of $100,000 in Total Owner Benefits. He also brags about his brilliant tax strategy that he got from inside a box of Cracker Jacks. ". . . It saves me on payroll taxes!" This is because he takes all his income from the firm on his K-1 (IRS Form 1065) as pure "profit." And that's why he's running around thinking his law firm has a 20% profit margin.

Lawyer Y: "Color Me Impressed" took $75,000 in K-1 profits. But she also took a $40,000 salary from the firm, and her C.P.A. allowed her to run $10,000 worth of expenses through the firm such as a car and a cell phone. Unfortunately, since she thinks narrowly and only thinks in terms of GAAP-compliant profits, Lawyer Y was so impressed with

Lawyer Z that she took some bad financial advice from him and made some poor hiring choices, too.

Which brings us to . . .

Lawyer X: "YOU." Yes, it is true, correct, and accurate that you and your tax strategist made some strategic decisions last year to arrange some of the firm's business affairs in such a way that it produced "only" a 10% profit. But you also took $50,000 in W-2 salary because you didn't get your tax strategy out of a box of popcorn. Instead, you work with a bookkeeper who doesn't suck. You work with an experienced law firm business management advisor. And you seek advice from a professional tax strategist. And together, your team of professional and experienced advisors helped you develop a legal, ethical, and intelligent proactive strategy that allowed the firm to incur $50,000 worth of expenses with pre-tax dollars, which benefited you, too. This brings YOUR Total Owner Benefits to $150,000, or 30% of the $500,000 gross revenue the firm produced.

Here's another example:

Example 2:

	Lawyer X ($500k gross revenue)	Lawyer Y ($500k gross revenue)	Lawyer Z ($500k gross revenue)
W-2 Earned Income	$75,000	$60,000	$50,000
K-1 Income	$25,000 (5% PROFIT)	$75,000 (15% PROFIT)	$100,000 (20% PROFIT)
Owner Benefits	$50,000	$15,000	$0
Total Owner Benefits	$150,000	$150,000	$150,000

Here, we see all three law firms each grossed the same amount because they attracted the same number of clients, delivered the same amount of value to those clients, but pursued different tax strategies. You'll notice that each firm's owner enjoyed the same Total Owner Benefits margin of 15%. But even though Mr. Bragadoccio is going around telling anyone who doesn't know any better that his firm had a 20% profit margin, YOU get to enjoy more purchasing power from your law firm because of some of the tax savings not represented in this illustration. So, Lawyer Z, let me ask you a question: Do you like apples?[13]

Taken together, what I hope these two examples help illustrate is why it is going to drive you crazy when you get together with other law firm owners at bar functions, or when you start talking with other law firm owners on discussion forums, and someone says, "My law firm is twice as profitable as your law firm because I've got 20% profits." Meanwhile, you're beating yourself up wondering what's wrong with you and your business, even though your Total Owner Benefits may be higher.

■ ■ ■

---

13 If you are very cool, like me, then you will instantly recognize this reference to a line from the movie, *Good Will Hunting* ☺

CHAPTER 10

IS IT OVERHEAD OR OVERHEAD?

Did you know that for thousands of years, the word "blue" didn't exist in any known language? And there's even evidence to suggest that without a word in their vocabulary to describe what my seven-year-old son can readily identify as his favorite color, our ancestors may not have even been able to discern the color blue.

In the late 1800s, a British scholar named William Gladstone was studying Homer's "The Odyssey" and noticed some unconventional descriptions of color. For instance, honey was described as green, while iron was called violet. However, no mention of blue existed.

A few years later, another scholar named Lazarus Geiger followed up on this observation by analyzing ancient Icelandic, Hindu, Chinese, Arabic, and Hebrew texts to see if they had a word for the color blue. He found no mention of the word "blue."

In fact, the first people to have a word for blue were the Egyptians. That was the first culture able to produce artificial blue dyes. From then, it seems awareness of the color spread throughout the modern world.

In 2015, psychologist Jules Davidoff published a paper based on an experiment conducted with the Himba tribe in Namibia. Their language has no distinct word for blue, though they had several words to describe different shades of green.

When asked to identify which square stood out from the rest (a single blue square among a group of green squares), they had extreme difficulty. As obvious as the blue square looks to us, the Himba people were unable to detect the blue square amongst the green squares.[14]

"So, what does any of this have to do with the overhead of my law firm?"

Well, here it is: I've been told that what I am about to share with you is revolutionary. And I sincerely hope that it resonates with you and that you'll join the revolution. And maybe one day in the future, this better way of accounting for overhead will be considered obvious to accountants everywhere:

There are Two Different Kinds of Overhead:
STATIC -VS- DYNAMIC

GAAP doesn't distinguish between Static vs. Dynamic Overhead. Consequently, most bookkeepers and even more C.P.A.s can't "see" it.

In the original *Profit First* book, Mike talks about the concept of "Overhead Expense." But it wasn't until he was sitting at my kitchen table (literally) that he says he had the "aha" moment when I described for him how we make this distinction with our clients and how much easier it suddenly becomes for my team to help them make their law firms so much more profitable.

---

14 Scan this QR code to see studies about the Himba people and their relationship with the color blue.

Let me explain.

Static Overhead is a category of overhead expenses that do not pay for themselves. Dynamic Overhead is a category of overhead expenses that do pay for themselves and continue to pay for themselves, especially as you scale the business.

While it may be true that not having "enough" Static Overhead will impede your ability to run your law firm and generate any profit at all, adding more Static Overhead won't necessarily make the law firm MORE profitable. Examples of Static Overhead include electricity, rent, dues, and subscriptions. Not feeding "enough" electricity to your law firm will have things grinding to a halt in a hurry. But adding more electricity won't tend to grow revenues or profits. Paying more in Bar dues doesn't add more value to your business than paying "just enough."

Dynamic Overhead is of a very different nature and must be treated accordingly if we are to maximize the profitability of your law firm. Most things related to marketing and sales and workflow efficiency are Dynamic in nature. The more (good) marketing your firm invests in, the more potentially profitable business you should expect. The more tools and training and support the firm provides for its staff, the more efficient the staff should become, thereby increasing the firm's capacity to be more productive and with an ever-improving Labor:Cost Ratio.[15] The more that management invests in proper financial controls and strategic planning, the more that opportunities for profits should be identified.

---

15 Greg Crabtree introduced me to this important Key Performance Indicator in his book, *Simple Numbers, Straight Talk, Big Profits!* (Crabtree, 2011). A law firm grosses $1MM with a total labor cost of $100,000. The Labor:Cost Ratio would be 10 (Total revenue/Total Labor Cost). If the firm were to invest in training (for example) and thereby produces $2MM with the same $10,000 Labor Cost the firm's ratio would improve to 20. **Find out what YOUR law firm's Labor:Cost Ratio is:**

The subject of "rent" comes up a lot in the context of this discussion, and it can get a bit tricky. Not giving your staff "enough" space to function will reduce productivity, and you'll need to add more space as your team grows. So, it may appear that adding more space causes your law firm to grow (build it and they will come); but, in fact, rent is also an example of Static Overhead in the sense that once your staff has "enough" space, giving them more space won't tend to make them any more productive or profitable. Rent can also get a bit tricky because the quality of the space tends to be tied to marketing, and "good marketing" is almost always an example of Dynamic Overhead. But once the firm has the appropriate quality of space in the right quantity to match its staff complement and brand, adding more space doesn't tend to drive revenues up.

Another example of Static Overhead that sometimes gets confusing is a firm's telephone and communication system. There is a minimum threshold for utility, and once that threshold is met, adding additional devices or more lines won't help generate a profit and is simply wasteful. But if you're expanding your firm's telephone system because you are kicking off a marketing campaign that requires your marketing team to conduct **a massive communication outreach campaign to reconnect with former clients** (hint, hint), then it probably makes a lot more dollars and sense to consider each dialer's line to be part of Dynamic Overhead.

Yes, you should be going through your Static Overhead expenses with a fine-tooth comb and cut whatever your firm doesn't need, just as Mike recommends in *Profit First*. But what you don't want to do is cut Dynamic Overhead because you mistakenly believed it to be Static in nature or can't tell the difference.

Law firm owners take bad advice from their bookkeepers and accountants all the time in this regard. I've had more knock-down, drag-out fights than I can count over these issues with bookkeepers and accountants I was paying for bad advice. That was until I learned to make the distinction between Static vs. Dynamic Overhead.

I'm pretty sure by now, you've got the point; but since this costly mistake gets made so often, I'm going to err on the side of caution and share another very obvious example that so many bookkeepers and financial accountants seem to miss, like the Himba people who didn't have a word for blue, so they couldn't see it.

Suppose you sit down towards the end of Q4 to work out a budget for the following year. Your first question ought to be, "How much in Total Owner Benefits do I want the firm to provide for my family and me?"

Then, you'd want to ask your team to help you calculate how much the firm must gross in order for you and your family to enjoy that level of Total Owner Benefits. In other words, start with the end in mind.

Example:

Step 1: "To live the way I want to live and not just settle for whatever I can get by on, the firm must produce $250,000 in Total Owner Benefits through a combination of my W-2 Salary, "profits" I'll report on my K-1 form, and other Owner Benefits that will enrich my life even though they'll technically be categorized as business expenses."

Step 2: "Given how aggressively we plan to grow the firm, our projected Labor:Cost Ratio and other expenses, we are figuring the firm ought to operate at about a 30% Total Owner Benefit Margin. $250,000/.33 = $750,000. So, our Gross Revenue Goal is $750,000 for next year."

Step 3: "Since our blended average case or matter value is $5,000, the firm needs to open, close and get paid for about 150 files next year." (750,000/5,000 = 150).

Step 4: "Since our sales conversion rate is about 50%, this means Marketing & Intake must deliver 24 prospects to Sales each month." ((150/12 = 12.5) / .50) = 24).

Step 5: "Our average case or matter remains open for about 6 months, which means we need a staff complement capable of managing about 75 open and active cases at all times, plus, the newly opened ones and the about-to-be-closed ones, which tend to require more attention."

Step 6: "Now that we know we will need enough people in acquisitions to generate, intake, and meet with 24 prospective new clients per month and enough people in production to open and close about 12 new cases per month, plus service an average of 75 open and active cases at all times, we can figure out how much staff we will need and how much space, equipment, and training they will need."

Step 7: "Now that we know how much marketing, sales, production, people, physical plant, and financial controls the firm will need in order to achieve the Owner's Financial Goals while respecting the Owner's Personal Goal of not becoming a prisoner to the firm and all while advancing the Owner's Professional Goal of using the work of the firm to make the world a better place in a way that matters to the Owner enough to go through all this trouble . . . now we can begin to develop a Business Plan."

You now understand the foundation upon which impressive success is built for the hundreds and hundreds of highly successful law firms that How To Manage A Small Law Firm helps manage. **Download a complimentary Business Plan Workbook** today.

Question: Is your C.P.A. walking you through any or all of these critical business management questions? Don't feel too bad if your C.P.A. and/or your bookkeeper aren't even asking you how much you want to earn from your business next year. As I've tried to explain throughout this book, that's not what Certified PUBLIC Accountants or bookkeepers are trained to do. They're not trained to be forward-looking strategic planners. They're not trained to be Law Firm Business Growth Advisors™.

Now consider this . . .

Let's suppose that we've figured out what we'd normally figure out by following the thought process I've shared above. And we've developed a marketing campaign that contemplates paying $1,000 for a marketing program with the expectation that it will produce $3,000 of new business. So, you give your bookkeeper and/or your C.P.A. your plan for the year. Except you notice that instead of that marketing program generating $3,000 of new business per month, it's producing $5,000 of new business each month.

Assuming you have the rest of your firm's 7 Main Parts working properly, what we'd want to do next is test to see if we invest $2,000, will it bring us back $10,000? If we invest $3,000, will it bring us back $15,000? If we invest $4,000, will it bring us back $20,000? If the ROI on your firm's "Marketing Overhead Expense" is scaling up like this or even close, then it's a Dynamic Expense. And we'd want to keep testing and clicking the dial up on this expense . . . right?

Can I tell you exactly how many financial accountants and bookkeepers I have had to battle to protect the profits of a law firm for an owner? No, I cannot because I have lost count. That's how many law firm owners I've met who were willing to just accept it when their bookkeeper or their C.P.A. told them that they had to "cut back" to keep the firm in alignment with its budget, seemingly blind to the fact that what they were "cutting back" on was feed for the golden goose! Remember the Himba people couldn't see the color blue until they learned the word "blue."

Another obvious example of Dynamic Overhead is sales. If you have one salesperson and most weeks, they're able to bring in $10,000 of new revenue for your firm, well, I wonder what happens if we invest more to train, manage, and support that one salesperson. What if we hire, train, and properly manage a second salesperson?

Sales is almost always Dynamic Overhead. If adding more salespeople or giving your sales team more and better training and management doesn't tend to improve their performance, chances are you have the wrong salespeople or the wrong people training and managing them. Lots of law firm owners who are inexperienced entrepreneurs mistakenly conclude that a category of overhead that's usually Dynamic isn't, simply because of poor hiring practices and/or poor management.

Unfortunately, very few bookkeepers and fewer C.P.A.s make the distinction between Static vs. Dynamic Overhead, and most mix them all together as "Overhead." This is why there are so many struggling law firms whose owners are busy chopping away at "Overhead" thinking they're going to make their law firm more profitable by eliminating waste—not knowing what they're really doing is cutting off their firm's potential for future growth. Now you won't be one of them!

Want to Learn Even More About This?

■ ■ ■

PART II

CHAPTER 11

WHAT A SMALL LAW FIRM BOOKKEEPER (WHO DOESN'T SUCK) SHOULD BE DOING FOR YOU

In this part of the book, I am going to spell out for you what a book-keeper who does NOT suck ought to be doing for your law firm and why it matters in terms of the profitability and predictability of revenues in your business and in your life.

I am going to lay out for you and help you understand the practical benefits of understanding certain key reports you ought to expect your bookkeeper to be delivering to you and walking you through each month.

You needn't have any formal training in the subject matter that follows in order to become a much more empowered and sophisticated consumer of bookkeeping services. I will be using plain English. I will be providing simple examples. You won't have to do any math at all. But if you're as bad at math as I am, you may enjoy the learning experience a bit more if you have a calculator easily within reach, just to help you follow along with some of the examples.

And I am going to explain the type of conversations your bookkeeper ought to be initiating with you about the financial reports of your business, which impact the lifestyle that you enjoy. Because I'm here to tell you that when done right, bookkeeping that does not suck can and should give you the tools and information you need to navigate your law firm to more profits today so that you can live a better life tomorrow.

If you'd prefer to just watch or listen or if you want to **explore these topics in more depth** and maybe get a different perspective here's something you might enjoy:

None of This is New:

To begin with, I want you to keep in mind that bookkeeping is not new. Records indicate that bookkeeping was in existence as early as 6,000 B.C. Historical artifacts show that nearly every ancient civilization had some form of financial and numerical record-keeping. In fact, many scholars believe the written word was invented by bookkeepers to keep track of financial transactions between traders. Historians have unearthed traces of commercial contracts in the ancient ruins of great kingdoms such as Babylon and archives that show systematic recordings of accounts from farm produce in ancient Greece as well as from the relatively modern Roman Empire.[16]

The software program your bookkeeper probably uses today is based on bookkeeping fundamentals that were first presented in the late 15th century by the Italian mathematician, Frater Luca Pacioli. In his book, *Everything About Arithmetic, Geometry, and Proportion*, Pacioli described

16 "How the World's First Accountants Counted on Cuneiform" https://www.bbc.com/news/business-39870485

Gary Previts, Peter Walton, and Peter Wolnizer. *A Global History of Accounting, Financial Reporting, and Public Policy* https://books.google.com/books?id=nhDu3CghZZgC&printsec=frontcover#v=onepage&q&f=false

in detail the accounting system still being used to manage businesses all over the world: the double-entry system, including the use of various bookkeeping instruments such as journals and ledgers.

Incidentally, despite the fact that most people give Pacioli credit as the father of modern bookkeeping and accounting, there is an ongoing debate between scholars and historians contesting Pacioli's double-entry system. It is claimed the double-entry system was in use for many gen-erations before Pacioli's publication. Opposers cite Benedetto Cotrugli's 1458 book, *Of Commerce and the Perfect Merchant*, as the first documented guide for the double-entry system to keep track of revenues, expenses, and profits. But since Pacioli is known to have been a personal friend of Leonardo da Vinci, it is Pacioli who usually gets the credit. So, you can add bookkeeping and influence to your list of things that do not change.

It may seem hard, but I want you to try and imagine what bookkeep-ing was like before computers. Spreadsheets were handwritten, humans did the arithmetic without calculators, paper ledgers were maintained by hand, and filing cabinets were the norm. The skills of a good bookkeeper have always been crucial. But before computers, it would have been laugh-able to even consider the possibility that a person could hold themselves out to be a bookkeeper without being able to demonstrate meticulous attention to detail, a good head for numbers, and a deep understanding of double-entry bookkeeping. This is because each financial transaction had to be recorded by hand on a ledger, and the risk of human error was high. So, the bookkeeper—the person whose job it was to "keep the books"—had to keep a sharp eye for potential problems and bring those potential problems to the attention of the client on a timely basis before the bookkeeper went and recorded several more pages by hand, in ink.

So, there was a time when it was safe to assume that one's bookkeeper—even if only out of self-interest—would be on the lookout for and proactively bring issues to the attention of their client. Otherwise, the bookkeeper might work for weeks or months recording several pages of records in ink, then they'd have to go back and correct their mistake, probably by candlelight. Getting a set of books that are "accurate" is a minimum. But if your bookkeeper today isn't charging enough to afford themselves the opportunity to initiate conversations with you each month and walk you through the financial reports they're producing in order to bring issues and trends and red flags to your attention, that's a problem (for you). Because that means you're missing out on the best parts of working with a bookkeeper who doesn't suck, namely Clarity, Insight, and Actionable Information.

So it was that—long before anyone had a computer to work with and email to hide behind—experts in the field of bookkeeping developed many of the same modern procedures the best bookkeepers still use today to help verify the accuracy of records and, importantly, help their clients understand and make sense of the financial records being kept about their businesses.

After all, what's the point of keeping financial records about your business if you're not looking at those financial reports that you are paying for? And what's the point of paying for and looking at financial reports if you're not using them to make better, more confident, and more profitable decisions based on what you can see is really happening in your business?

Unfortunately, nowadays it seems anyone who can operate a software program can (and they do) go around calling themselves a bookkeeper. And even more unfortunately, lawyers who never took even a single course on bookkeeping or accounting fall for it. Because they don't know the difference. Now you do.

> *The Most Profitable Law Firms*
> **WOULDN'T BE**
> *The Most Profitable Law Firms*
> **WITHOUT BOOKKEEPERS**
> **WHO DON'T SUCK**

There are many reasons why most—not all—small law firms are usually so much less profitable and so much more stressful to run than large law firms. But undoubtedly, one of the contributing factors is that decision-makers in large law firms have the benefit of timely data and relevant reports, which help them see further into the future than do owners of most small law firms, due to the aforementioned sucky bookkeeping.

Owners and the management of larger law firms are thereby empowered to make more well-informed and more confident decisions as compared to the owners of most small law firms, who are often only working with murky information that forces them to be thinking and planning only weeks or months ahead.

Can you even IMAGINE how much better that might feel? How much more CONFIDENCE you could be enjoying as a business owner? How much more PROFITABLE your law firm has the potential to be? Don't just imagine. **Watch, listen and learn from these small law firm owners** about how they did it and how you can do it too:

The problem, of course, is that too many small law firm owners have bookkeepers who suck. And by "suck," I mean that they suck the life and fun and confidence out of the law firms they serve, along with the profits, and leave the owner with disappointment and frustration. I don't mean that these bookkeepers are incompetent or that they are producing inaccurate financial reports, though we see plenty of that, too, when we take over the bookkeeping of so many small law firms.

What I mean is that those bookkeepers suck because they produce misleading or irrelevant financial reports. The reports might be accurate, but they're not useful. So, I say that a bookkeeper "sucks" when they don't produce the right financial reports that you need to confidently navigate the unfamiliar terrain ahead when it comes to growing your small law firm. And I say that they suck when they consider their job done when they press "send" on the email, which delivers your law firm's financial reports to your inbox each month, instead of insisting upon a call or web meeting to walk you through your firm's financials to be sure you actually understand and feel empowered to make smart decisions based on what's in there.

To illustrate this point, I want to ask you to please try to imagine you're heading out into the wild, with a set of maps but without any guidance from the mapmaker to spot the hidden dangers they ought to know about, since they made the map. And as you are falling off a very high cliff that your mapmaker knew or should have known was there, you call up to the mapmaker who sold you the map:

**"WHY DIDN'T YOU WARN ME
ABOUT THIS HIDDEN CLIFF?"**

And they call back as you fall:

**"BECAUSE YOU DIDN'T WANT TO PAY
A LITTLE BIT MORE
FOR THE ADVICE."**

And as you continue falling, you call back:

**"I'm so disappointed you didn't care enough about me to tell me that
for a little bit more, you could have not only sold me a fuller & more
complete set of maps... but you'd have also been willing to take the
time to warn me about things like this cliff so that I could reach my
goals faster, with more confidence & less stress...
instead of falling down this cliff...
YOU SUUUUUUCCCKKKKKK...."**

(Yes, it was a very high cliff.)

But I'm not even talking about the software operators who hold themselves out as bookkeepers. Most of them are just incompetent and don't even know what they don't know. I'm talking about most of the bookkeepers out there who do know better. And they totally suck because they're content to deliver an incomplete set of financials for you to figure out on your own[17]—even though they know, or they would know (if they cared enough to ask), that you are heading out into that unfamiliar territory with your whole family loaded up into the wagon with you!

I need to repeat this: A well-meaning bookkeeper who is simply incompetent could be forgiven. They should be avoided, of course. But they can be forgiven, for they know not what they do to their clients. That's not what I'm talking about! What I'm talking about is the fact that there are hundreds of thousands of small law firms that are under-performing their full potential. And the owners of those law firms are working harder than they might otherwise have to work to make up the difference. Because their bookkeepers do not care enough about them to double or even triple their bookkeeping fee to increase the value delivered by tenfold.

Now, before you think I'm being too judgmental, let me tell you why I am so worked up about this. It's because this is exactly what happened to me! I was working my ass off and growing my business, but I wasn't taking home any of the profits. And I never knew what was waiting for me or my business around the next corner. And I was always stressed out and worried about cash flow. So yes, I get pretty riled up about this stuff. Because I know from personal experience how bad it can be. And I know from personal experience how much better life can be when your bookkeeper doesn't suck, which is why I created Small Law Firm

---

17 Having a monthly call to ask you a bunch of technical questions about which account to book some expenses to is NOT a substitute for having a meaningful discussion with you which ends with you feeling empowered because you actually understand the financials of your business.

106

Bookkeeping That Does Not Suck. As of the date of this writing, it is currently the largest and the fastest-growing bookkeeping service in the world created by lawyers for lawyers, instead of by C.P.A.s who are sworn to protect the public instead of you.

■ ■ ■

CHAPTER 12

THE KEY FINANCIAL REPORTS EVERY SMALL LAW FIRM BOOKKEEPER WHO DOES NOT SUCK OUGHT TO INSIST UPON WALKING YOU THROUGH EACH MONTH

Have *you ever stopped to seriously consider* what separates some of the most financially profitable small law firms from the ones that just do okay? The (small) differences may surprise you. Discovery of these small changes that you have significant control over sure do disappoint all the excuse-makers who are comforted by a false belief that there are major and insurmountable differences between the most profitable vs. the least profitable law firms out there in any given practice area and in any given market.

But the differences are really few. One of these differences is that the owners of the most financially profitable law firms pay attention to things that the owners of the least financially profitable law firms do not pay attention to. And you get some of what you pay for with your money, but you get a lot more of what you pay for with your attention. So please, pay close attention to the lessons that follow. It truly can change your life for the better. Invest your full attention for about one hour and see if it doesn't give you some valuable insights—or at least some important questions you can put to your bookkeeper and/or the rest of your business management advisor(s).[18] The presence or absence, and the quality, of each one of the following concepts could increase or decrease the amount of profit you take from your law firm by as much as one full percentage point annually.

One percent may not seem like a lot. But let me tell you, it adds up. It's true! The explanation for the difference between a law firm that returns 15% net operating income (profit) vs. the law firm that merely pays the owner's salary for services rendered but never gives the owner or their family any financial profits on top of that can be largely found in the explanations that follow. If you take each concept individually and just go one by one, it's going to be a lot easier and quite liberating. You are a couple of hours away from knowing more about what to look for in a bookkeeper and how to extract maximum value from the bookkeeping services you pay for than almost any other lawyer you know. Unless they have read this book, of course. I think that's pretty exciting!

Now, before we dive into the last batch of substantive lessons of this book, I want to take a moment to congratulate you for the progress you have made. It says something very positive about you that you even picked up a book like this and even more that you are committed enough to your own full potential to read this far. It's not easy. And in case no one else in your life is saying it, I want to say, "Thank you."

I am thanking you for trusting me enough to read and consider what I have had to say throughout these pages. If you will permit me to be so

---

18 One of the things the most successful law firm owners of all shapes, sizes and practice areas all have in common is that **they invest their time with business management advisors** to bring objectivity, accountability and perspective to their decisions.

bold, I want to thank you on behalf of your future self, too. You will soon wake up with a more profitable law firm and a better life because of the work you are doing today.

I'd imagine you already feel something beginning to make a shift inside of you from having only learned about these concepts and ideas.

Now imagine, just 12 short months from now, how much better your life has become because you will act upon these lessons and put them to use in your law firm and in your life.

So, as I said, thank you.

■ ■ ■

This is a QR code that will take you to a page where you can **listen to and watch some of our Bookkeepers Who Do Not Suck walking some of our actual small law firm owners through their financials.**

This way, you will be able to hear the following concepts in action. Because until you hear it for yourself, it may be difficult to appreciate what you might be missing out on. As you will hear, the conversations are not "scripted." Every situation is unique, but they do all tend to follow this basic logic. Once you and your bookkeeper get into a "rhythm," it will take about 90 very profitable minutes once a month to cover the following items:

1. Key Performance Indicators

2. Gross Revenues

3. Cash Flow Projections

4. Cash On Hand—Including Profit First Accounts

5. A/R, IOLTA Balance & Lines of Credit

6. Profitability

7. Balance Sheet (with special emphasis on changes in equity)

8. Budget Variance Report

9. Accounts Receivable (Yes, we are going to want to discuss this topic, twice.)

10. Open/Close Case Ratio

11. Average Case Value

12. Average Case Calendar Time

13. Cost of Acquisition

14. Labor Cost Ratio

15. ROI (per direct revenue producer)

16. Core Working Capital

17. Trust Account Balance(s)

18. Wrap-Up: Clarification by your bookkeeper as to where some of the leaves and branches belong on some of the trees in the forest you are creating.

GOOD NEWS: This is all common sense. There's no complicated math involved. Yes, I know I said that already. Remember, I am a lawyer, too. And so, I know how scared most lawyers get any time the subject of math comes up. This is precisely why so many law firm owners struggle so much when it comes to the financial management of their business. But you don't have to know hardly anything about bookkeeping or accounting to become very effective in your use of these important financial concepts and ideas. And for the third time, you won't be asked to do any math!

So, take a deep breath and prepare to have your eyes opened wide to the impressive potential for profit likely all around you in your law firm.

■ ■ ■

CHAPTER 13

THE BASICS

1. **K**ey Performance Indicators (**KPIs**)—In every business, there are certain "shortcuts" you can use to get and keep a handle on what's happening in the business. At How To Manage A Small Law Firm, we help the law firms that we manage to set up a dashboard that shows them "at a glance" whether the KPIs they've decided to track are on-track (green light), a little off-track (yellow light), or if they're far enough off-track to warrant timely attention (red light).

The selection of KPIs is a lot like the selection of toppings at the ice cream parlor. There's something for everyone. And you don't want to overdo it with your ice cream toppings or your KPIs. In fact, when it comes to KPIs, the best number is one. Ideally, we want to be able to help you boil down your whole understanding of what's happening in your business to just one number.

The whole topic of how to use KPIs and dashboards to scale up your law firm could be the topic of its own book. So, instead of giving you a false sense of having learned all you need to know on this fascinating and fun subject (I'm not joking, it's actually pretty cool), I'll just share the following observations.

Key Performance Indicators aren't meant to give you a conclusion. They're meant to act as a warning light that lets you know when and where you should be paying extra attention in your business. All that it tells you when you see a green light is that everything appears to be going pretty close to the way we had expected. A yellow light means things are a little off but still within tolerable limits. And a red light means we should stop right away and figure out what's causing the red light so we can fix it before the machine breaks down.

Keep in mind, the fact that there's a variance between what was expected and planned for and what's now showing up in reality isn't always a bad thing. It's just different. And we should always pay attention when things are going differently than we had planned or expected. For example, let's say we expected gross revenues to be $100,000 for the month. If gross revenues for any given month were within 10% up or down, it's probably no big deal. If revenues are "off" by 20%, you may be seeing the beginnings of a deeper problem we can dig into and fix before it gets worse. And if your law firm's revenues are off by more than 30% in either direction in any given month, that tells us at least one of several things—all of which warrant immediate attention:

It can be that our original assumptions upon which our projections were based were wrong. If our assumptions were correct, then perhaps there's a flaw in our plan. If our plan is sound, then maybe someone isn't sticking to the plan. If everyone has remained faithful to the plan, then someone may need some training in how they're executing the plan. Or it could be a combination of these causes, or it could be something else that's causing the effect we see showing up on the dashboard.

So, the first thing you probably want to do each month is meet with your law firm's CFO to look at KPIs—and if you don't have a CFO helping you to manage, analyze, and understand what is happening in your business, then you should at least have a bookkeeper who is good enough to help you review your dashboard every month to be sure you're paying attention to issues and warning signals before it's too late.

Keep in mind, there is a BIG difference between what a bookkeeper does vs. what a CFO does. The long story short is that a bookkeeper looks backward at what has already happened. Your bookkeeper dutifully records history and prepares and presents reports to show you what has happened, ideally in a format that is intuitive and on a timely enough basis for you to act. A CFO analyzes the data and the reports that your bookkeeper prepares. A CFO helps you figure out why the variances are happening and how to maximize the good ones and what to do to improve the bad ones.

A CFO uses the reports prepared by your bookkeeper as a starting point to help you navigate into a better future. Plus, unless you happen to have been a CFO in a prior life, there's a very good chance that a CFO is going to be able to see things in the data that you and your bookkeeper are not trained to see. One of the big claims to fame for How To Manage A Small Law Firm is our "timeshare" CFO service that brings big-law-firm-level CFO services to solo and small law firms that could otherwise never have access to a high-caliber and experienced CFO. And a big part of the reason why we started Small Law Firm Bookkeeping That Does Not Suck is precisely because of all the sucky bookkeepers whose sucky bookkeeping kept interfering with our CFOs' ability to help our members analyze, interpret, and make profitable plans for their future. Remember, garbage in = garbage out. So, in order to be useful, your law firm's dashboard must be populated with reliable data. That reliable data comes from your bookkeeper (who hopefully does not suck).[19]

2. Gross Revenues—Top-line gross revenue is a pretty reliable reflection of how much value your law firm produces and delivers to its clients.

---

19 Please follow this link for **a more detailed explanation of the difference(s) between what you should expect from a good bookkeeper vs. a good controller vs. a good financial accountant vs. a good CFO** (management accountant):

Law firms produce gross revenue by marketing, selling, and delivering value to clients.

But the *timing* of when your law firm produces and delivers value to its clients, when the firm incurs the costs for producing that value, and when the firm gets paid can be the difference between a rich and rewarding life full of confidence and professional satisfaction or a life of stress and anxiety that so many small law firm owners unwittingly accept as being "normal."

If you're like most small law firm owners, the first thing you want to hear from your bookkeeper is how much top-line gross revenue was projected, expected, and planned for in the month just ended and year to date vs. how much was actually collected.

Lower than expected gross revenues could point to:

- Marketing problems—Not enough leads or poor-quality leads

- Sales problems—Poor conversion or follow-up with prospects, or the person handling the sales could be pathologically undercharging and/or over-committing the firm

- Production problems—Is the firm understaffed, has the staff been properly trained, is anyone managing the staff to ensure they're working on the right things at the right time, or are we just trusting them to self-manage?

- Problems with financial controls—Are we overworking the clients' individual ledger card balance(s) in the trust account? Do we have fixable problems with the firm's accounts receivable protocols? If it's a contingency firm, do we need to install a better case screening system or more proactive case management system to ensure timely prosecution of cases so they don't stall out?

THE POINT IS: "More clients" isn't usually the only or necessarily the most profitable button, switch, or dial to mess with when gross
revenues are down.

3. Cash Flow Projection—Each month, you probably want to know if
your firm will have enough cash on hand to meet its obligations (including its
financial obligations to you) every week for each of the next six to eight weeks.

A word about Cash Flow vs. Profitability . . . I recall the owner of a
multimillion-dollar law firm whose firm had positive cash flow. Yay! But
the law firm was slowly going out of business because it was losing about
$100,000 each month. And the owner didn't even know it!

Remember, cash flow is a measure of how much cash comes in and
how much cash goes out. The seven-figure law firm owner who was in my
office kept insisting that his law firm was profitable *"because all my bills
are getting paid and I'm getting my salary."* But what was really happening
was that the firm's administrator and bookkeeper had the firm incurring
liabilities all over the place to maintain its positive cash flow. The firm
was bringing in cash from its line of credit. It was collecting flat fees from
clients and incurring liabilities to deliver the work later. And the firm was
reducing cash disbursements and simply booking liabilities to staff for
earned bonuses and other inevitable expenses that would soon come due.

No, positive cash flow does not guarantee that a law firm is necessarily
profitable. But so long as your firm has positive cash flow, you can stay in
the game—long enough to turn things around. This is why the second
thing you probably want to know from your bookkeeper is, *"Will the firm
have enough cash on hand to meet its financial obligations each week—including its financial obligations to me—for each of the next six to eight weeks?"*

When the answer is "yes," you can relax and think your way through
almost any other problem the firm may be having. When the answer is
"no," then figuring out how to turn the answer to this important question
into a "yes" must become your top priority.

Keep in mind, there are many ways to solve cash flow problems in a small law firm. Debt is only one of the tools available to an experienced law firm management professional. This subject is too important to give it only a sentence or two in this book. Rather than distract you from the rest of this book about why and how to implement Profit First Bookkeeping in your law firm (which will help with cash flow, too), **I've included some additional resources specific to this subject here:**

4. Cash on Hand—How much cash do we have in our operating account? How much cash do we have sitting in the IOLTA? How much cash do we have stashed away in our various sinking funds including, and especially, my Profit First Accounts?

Gross Revenues tend to be the very first thing most entrepreneurs have an emotional need to know about. It's almost like we can't even think about anything else until we know what the firm grossed in the last month, quarter, or year to date. Then, your mind probably shifts to, "Oh no, but what about tomorrow?" So, our small law firm bookkeepers who do not suck talk about cash flow projections each month with the law firm owners whose law firms we serve. And then, we know from experience that the third thing you want to know is how much cash your law firm has on hand. Because with enough cash, we can solve (or survive long enough to find a solution to) almost any law firm management challenge.

If this is how your mind works, you are not alone. The team at How To Manage A Small Law Firm (which shares common ownership with Bookkeeping That Does Not Suck) has worked with thousands of solo and small law firm owners. Our clients have gross revenues ranging from start-ups ($0) to tens of millions of dollars. And neither the size of the firm nor the practice area, or even which flavor ice cream the owner(s) of the firm prefer, seems to change this way of thinking amongst the most successful small law firm owners. So, if you think this way, too, then we think you are in good company!

SINKING FUNDS

The technical definition of a "sinking fund" is a fund formed by periodically setting aside money for the gradual repayment of a debt or replacement of a wasting asset. The idea behind Profit First is that you deserve to pay yourself first, as the owner and lead investor in your business. But the mechanics upon which the implementation of Profit First depend require the use of a series of sinking funds.

If you've already read *Profit First*, you already know about the CAP account and the tax account and all the other separate sinking funds Mike recommends and which a Profit First Certified Bookkeeper will help you set up, protect, and keep track of. But the list Mike provides in *Profit First* is not exhaustive.

In a law firm, for example, it's a smart idea to set a little bit of money aside each month for the scheduled replacement of equipment. This way, you don't find your firm losing tens of thousands of dollars each month as production grinds to a halt at $500/hour all because you're trying to make some piece of old equipment last "just a little bit longer." It's so much easier to make the rational choice about equipment replacement when you've got a separate sinking fund with money already set aside and allocated just for that purpose.

As the owner of a law firm, it would also be wise to ask your book-keeper to help you set up a sinking fund for the addition or replacement of staff positions. We have seen far too many law firms stall out because the owner is afraid to dig into their pocket to "fund" the start-up of a new associate position or the addition of a new management position which, if properly recruited, onboarded, and trained, could become a highly profitable position within 90 days. Except, the owner never wants to lay out the 90 days plus the cost of a good recruiter. And so, instead of ever experiencing the very profitable benefits of having a professional legal administrator (for example), the growth and profitability of the law firm just languishes while the owner slowly burns out.

And if you really want to supercharge the growth of your law firm, imagine what would happen if you were to create a sinking fund for marketing and allocate a percentage of every case the firm opens to a marketing account.

Imagine what it would force you to do for your law firm if the only way the money could ever come out of that account is to invest it in marketing! A little growth would lead to a little more growth. And a little more growth would soon lead to even more growth. This, by the way, is one of the "secrets" we use to supercharge the growth of the law firms we help to manage at How To Manage A Small Law Firm. I put "secrets" in quotes because it's not exactly a secret since I've been standing on stages advocating for this practice since about 1999, when I first reported for duty as a Small Law Firm Business Management Advisor with the Florida Bar's Law Office Management Assistance Service (LOMAS).

Hopefully, your bookkeeper does not suck and has been talking with you about using sinking funds to help you grow your business, achieve your financial goals, and protect your sanity along the way.

5. A/R, IOLTA Balance, and Lines of Credit—If your review of the firm's cash flow projections show that the firm is headed toward a cash crunch and the firm doesn't have enough cash on hand, then the very best way to avert disaster is by getting serious about collecting A/R.

Accounts Receivable: Remember, by the time the money becomes part of the firm's accounts receivable, the costs to do the work have already been incurred and probably paid. So, every dollar of A/R that you collect can usually be deployed to solve or avoid whatever problems await. And it doesn't have to be paid back! Plus, when you are smart about how you go about collecting your firm's A/R, it tends to trigger more referrals and more repeat business from the client(s) who may (finally) begin to respect the firm, just a little bit more.

IOLTA: No A/R to collect? Good for you! Then how about the IOLTA? Remember, your clients gave you that money to hold in your trust account because they had a problem or an opportunity they were hoping the firm would solve for them. Your client does not want their money languishing in your law firm's trust account while their problem(s) persist. What they want is for your law firm to earn that money by solving their problem(s) for them, and the sooner, the better, as far as most of your clients are concerned!

By re-prioritizing the work to be done, we can often accomplish two worthwhile objectives at once: (1) We can accelerate the transfer of cash from the firm's IOLTA to the operating account, which may solve the firm's cash flow problem; and (2) We often make the client happier because we can demonstrate progress toward solving their problem(s)!

Credit: It is critical that each month you check the status of your law firm's credit facilities to be sure no one has been quietly putting you into debt without you recognizing what is happening until it's too late.

Of course, if you have established proper financial controls in your business, then your management team won't be able to incur debt for the firm without you knowing about it. Because you'll have to approve every transaction. But then, you will forget. Believe me, you will forget. And then one day, you will wake up thinking you have a few hundred thousand dollars' worth of credit left to use as a cushion in case you need it. Except you forgot that nine months ago, your office manager asked you to approve a small draw on the firm's line of credit. And seven months ago, you decided to make another small draw instead of picking up the phone to call and collect some of the firm's A/R. And then, five months ago . . . (you get the idea).

This is exactly how I woke up one day ten years ago with my line of credit completely tapped out. It rarely happens all at once. And it's really, really easy to forget about each of the little draws you made yesterday, especially when you're busy thinking about the exciting future ahead and putting out fires today. This is why I want you to insist upon seeing a report from your bookkeeper showing the firm's status with each creditor every month.

- What's our current balance?

- How much do we have left untapped?

- What's the interest rate?

- What is the status of our plan to retire the debt? ESPECIALLY if the creditor is your own household!

And in the case of a revolving line of credit, you better be sure you know how long it's going to be until the bank will require you to clear the line for 30 days.

For a much more complete discussion on why, whether, when, and how to make smart strategic use of debt as a ladder (instead of as a crutch), please follow this link:

6. Profitability—Are we making any progress, and if so, how much? In other words, *"Is all this trouble even worth it?!?!"*

Profitability shows up in two places: on the Profit &/or Loss Statement; but as we will discover a few pages from now, the most sophisticated entrepreneurs look to the Balance Sheet to determine if their law firm is truly making a profit.

At its most basic level, your firm's Profit &/or Loss Statement simply tells you:

How much revenue was collected but not necessarily earned (cash basis), or earned but not necessarily collected (accrual basis)

-vs.-

How much expense the firm incurred and paid out (cash basis), or incurred but the firm may not have actually paid it out yet (accrual basis). In other words, revenues as compared to expenses.

CASH BASIS VS. ACCRUAL BASIS ACCOUNTING: A VERY BRIEF PRIMER

Unless you have studied accounting, the important differences between cash-basis accounting vs. accrual-basis accounting can be a bit confusing. I still have to stop and think it through sometimes when my CFO takes me deep into the weeds.

Cash-basis accounting recognizes cash on the P&L when the cash is received, even if it has not yet been earned. If we receive cash, it counts as revenue, even if we owe work to the client. And we recognize an expense when we actually pay it, not when we first incur it. That's cash-basis accounting in a nutshell.

In fact, it is precisely because most small law firms operate on a cash-basis that Bar rules require you to hold unearned cash in your trust account. This isn't the only reason for having a trust account, of course, but one of the main reasons is to try and "force" your cash-basis accounting system to function more like an accrual basis accounting system.

An accrual-basis accounting system only recognizes revenue on the P&L after the cash is earned, regardless of when it may have been collected.

In the event that a law firm operating on an accrual-basis accounting system receives cash in the form of a flat fee that is "earned upon receipt," it obviously cannot be placed in the IOLTA, or else you'd be commingling funds.

So, what we do in accrual accounting with the cash that's legally earned, but when we still owe the work, is we record the cash as an asset on the balance sheet, and we record the costs we expect to incur to deliver the work on the balance sheet, too, but as a liability.

There are many factors to consider when making the decision whether to run your law firm on a cash-basis or on an accrual-basis accounting system.

Unless you're in Canada. Everywhere else, you will find most small law firms grossing less than about $10 million dollars per year are best served by using cash-basis accounting, for the sake of simplicity and for important tax reasons, too, which are too complex to get into in this book.

For the sake of simplicity, unless otherwise stated, all examples in this book and in the bonus materials are expressed in terms of cash accounting.

A more complete discussion about some of the very important differences, pros and cons, and to help you **decide when and how your law firm's books should be switched over from cash basis to accrual basis** can be found here:

To help you better appreciate the value you could be missing out on if your bookkeeper isn't taking the time to be sure to walk you through your law firm's P&L each month, let's take a look at the P&Ls of two different law firms:

Law Firm A has ONE HUNDRED THOUSAND DOLLARS ($100,000) cash sitting in its operating account. Law Firm A generates NINETY THOUSAND DOLLARS ($90,000) in monthly revenue. It pays out NINETY-FIVE THOUSAND DOLLARS ($95,000) in monthly expenses.

Law Firm B has just TEN THOUSAND DOLLARS ($10,000) cash in its operating account. Law Firm B generates NINETY-FIVE THOUSAND DOLLARS ($95,000) in monthly revenue. It pays out NINETY THOUSAND DOLLARS ($90,000) in monthly expenses.

Which law firm would YOU rather be the owner of? This is obviously a rhetorical question. Because all things being equal, Law Firm A will be out of business in 20 months ($100,000 cash on hand / $5,000 in monthly losses = 20 months until kapow!), whereas in that same period of time, Law Firm B will have produced $100,000 of profit, which can be taken out of the firm and protected in the owner's separate personal bank account or loaned back to the firm with a note, a repayment plan, and interest to give a profitable business more core working capital for ongoing growth and expansion. When you know your business is profitable, you don't mind being its bank.

Here's another very real-world example. Let's say you have the choice of being the owner of only one or the other of these two law firms:

Law Firm X has ONE HUNDRED THOUSAND DOLLARS ($100,000) cash in its operating account. It collected NINETY THOUSAND DOLLARS ($90,000) in revenue last month. It paid out NINETY-FIVE THOUSAND DOLLARS ($95,000) in monthly expenses last month.

Law Firm Y has ZERO ($0) cash in its operating account. It generated revenues of NINETY-FIVE THOUSAND DOLLARS ($95,000) last month. It paid out expenses of NINETY THOUSAND DOLLARS ($90,000) last month. But this law firm has access to a line of credit. Let's say this law firm has access to a $50,000 revolving line of credit.

Question 1: All things being equal, which law firm would you rather own? Obviously, it's Law Firm Y. At least it is generating a profit each month.

Question 2: Would it be smarter to use Law Firm Y's credit to even out cash flow and pay it all back in, let's say, 10 months, or don't take the credit and live on the edge every month for the next 10 months?

Without a P&L you might sentence yourself to a year of misery. But by consulting the firm's P&L over the past several months, we can see a clear pattern of profitable months, not just months with positive cash flow. We are now empowered to make choices that can free up much-needed energy, which empowers us to focus on marketing or process improvements that may further contribute to profitability and growth.

And Now (Drumroll, Please) Enter, the Balance Sheet . . .

7. **Balance Sheet**—The real arbiter of profitability is the Balance Sheet because it tells us if all our efforts are building any equity in the business or if we're just treading water.

You already understand how a balance sheet works.

Consider a house you buy at fair market value for $100,000 with a 10% down payment. The property is worth $100,000, and after your down payment there's a $90,000 mortgage. This leaves $10,000 of equity. Pretty simple, right?

Okay, let's suppose property values increase in the area and the house is now worth $110,000. The mortgage is still $90,000, right? Your equity in the house just went up to $20,000: your original $10,000 down payment and $10,000 from appreciation. Makes sense, yes?

Alright, now let's suppose you take it upon yourself to repaint the whole house, which brings the value up to $120,000. The mortgage is still $90,000. How much equity did your efforts add to your house balance sheet (assets – liabilities = equity). By picking up a paint brush and painting the house, you added $10,000 of equity. Your equity in the house is now $30,000. Your original deposit gave you the first $10,000 of equity in the property; appreciation produced another $10,0000 of equity; and your industry produced another $10,000 of equity.

Someday, you're going to sell that house. And someday, you may decide to sell your law firm, too. When either of these two days arrive, what you're going to care about the most is how much equity you get to walk away from the closing table with. This is why more sophisticated law firm owners want to see their firm's balance sheet to know if equity is increasing or decreasing each month due to the management decisions they are making in and about the business.

"Are we making a profit? Are we making any progress toward making a profit? Is all of this going to be worth it?"

After the first two questions are satisfied and you know you're on it, or can see the path to profitability, then we can dive more deeply into some of the much more interesting details. This is where we go to find clues and opportunities to grow your business even more!

Some lawyers (too many lawyers) mistakenly believe that a law firm cannot be sold. Most of these lawyers do not understand the difference between a P&L and a Balance Sheet. For a more complete lesson on **why and how a law firm can be valued and sold**, please follow this link:

■ ■ ■

CHAPTER 14

FOR WHEN YOU REALLY TAKE PROFITS SERIOUSLY

8. **B**udget Variance Report—This is a comparison between what you were expecting to happen vs. what did actually happen in reality. Consider how useless the following piece of information is:

"Your law firm grossed $100,000 last month."

Your mind is screaming for an answer to this question right now:

"COMPARED TO WHAT?!?!?!"

If you were expecting and planning for the law firm to gross $50,000 and it grossed twice that much, you might be happy at first. But then, you'd probably begin to wonder, "Why? How?"

You might think to yourself, "In my experience, estimates are usually a little off but not usually by 100%. I wonder if there might be a problem with the accuracy of this information. I should probably investigate."

And then, you might discover that last month was a short month. So, all of last month's revenue got booked to this month. And year to date, you're exactly on track. Okay, no problem. No worries. Keep on truckin'!

Or you might discover that marketing plan you had such high hopes for . . . holy frijoles, *it actually worked!* And now you're about to have a whole new set of problems because if you don't act fast to gear up production, you're about to have a whole bunch of unhappy clients and/or you're going to burn out your staff.

By studying your firm's Budget Variance Report, you might also discover that year to date, the firm is on track—yaaay!—but that your law firm has a natural cash flow cycle where there are a few unprofitable months followed by a big "make-up" month. And the pattern repeats itself, like Old Faithful in Yellowstone National Park.

If this is what you discover, then the next time you're in the middle of a "down" cycle, perhaps you won't make a bunch of self-defeating decisions like cutting back on marketing, laying off staff whom you'll need again soon, and scaring the crap out of your family by telling them the sky is falling when, in fact, your firm is just in the middle of a down cycle. But year to date, everything is exactly on track.

Or maybe you'll **reach out to an experienced law firm business management advisor** for help to identify opportunities to smooth out the cycle:

A Budget Variance Report gives you context. It also points the way and helps identify small problems early before they become big problems and big opportunities you might not otherwise notice until it's too late and therefore miss out on. To illustrate, let's take two common examples of the sort of "intelligence" that is often found when a bookkeeper who does not suck cares enough to charge a little bit more so they can afford to invest the time required to walk you through your law firm's financials.

TOTALLY TRUE STORY #1:

One of our clients gave an employee a gas card to help with the employee's long commute. Based on mileage, fuel prices, and the efficiency of the employee's vehicle we projected the expense to the firm would be about $150 per month. Covering expenses for employees is often a much more profitable approach than merely giving raises. But after a few months, something stood out. The variance was growing—and not in the right direction.

After five months, when the monthly variance grew to 100%, an investigation was begun. Keep in mind, a 100% variance on a $150/month cost might raise fewer red flags than a much smaller 20% variance on a $10,000 monthly line item. It all depends on scale.

In any event, after seeing a five-month trend, the investigation was begun, and it ruled out the following potential explanations: Fuel prices hadn't doubled. The employee was still driving the same vehicle. The employee had not moved farther away from the office. And the employee didn't appear to be misusing the gas card by purchasing fuel for family and friends.

As a last resort, we sent the employee to a trusted mechanic. What we discovered was that there was a puddle of fuel directly underneath the rear seat above the fuel tank. A consistent "trickle" of gasoline was dripping down under the vehicle. It turned out there was a leak in the sending unit at the top of the gas tank. Between the gasoline that was leaking out and lost efficiency from the depressurized fuel tank (the mechanic explains it better than me), that accounted for all the extra fuel being consumed. Oh, and by the way, a potentially life-threatening situation was identified and resolved, thanks to clues provided by the law firm's budget variance report.

(I can't make this stuff up.)

TOTALLY TRUE STORY # 2:

Another ambitious law firm owner brought us in to analyze her law firm and ". . . figure out why the hell my law firm isn't growing!"

One of the line items in the budget that showed up on the Budget Variance Report was the firm's "Marketing Expense." We noticed there was no variance in the firm's marketing expense. It was projected to be X, and it was exactly X every month. In fact, the firm's controller (a person who had never grown a business before) was proud when he reported that he kept a tight rein on expenses, and he was eager to review the firm's Budget Variance Report, which he and the firm's bookkeeper prepared and sent to the owner each month.

"We notice the marketing expense is exactly spot-on each month with what you projected at the end of last year for this year," we said.

"Yes, we keep a tight rein on expenses around here," the firm's controller and bookkeeper responded together with glee.

"We see that you're also tracking ROI on several different marketing channels," we said.

"Yes, and we're keeping those in line, too," they replied with enthusiasm.

I'll spare you the rest of my sad attempts at writing dialogue and get to the point. The law firm's controller and bookkeeper had cut off funds to one of the firm's marketing channels because actual expenses had more than doubled over projections. More specifically, the firm had begun a program whereby non-attorney employees were encouraged and reimbursed for costs related to their attending networking events to magnify the firm's presence in the local market. It turned out the program was more popular than anyone could have imagined. And so now, "to keep a tight rein on costs," the firm's finance department was regularly and routinely denying employee requests for approval to attend networking events to represent the firm.

As a result, morale was in decline, and employees were beginning to doubt the sincerity of the owner's commitment to growth. Plus, it turned out that it was quite a profitable program for the firm, giving a handsome ROI for every dollar (even every dollar over budget) invested.

By the time we found and fixed the problem (we simply updated the projections on this dynamic overhead expense), we calculated that the firm had likely missed out on several hundred thousand dollars of profitable new referral business, all because the financials were being given to the owner, but she wasn't being walked through her firm's financials to be sure she really understood what was happening in the business. Once we helped the owner of this law firm understand what the Budget Variance Report was trying to tell her, to her credit, she instantly connected the dots and approved the revisions to the budget. As a result, more networking requests were approved, morale improved, and the firm saw a very nice ROI on this particular marketing initiative.

9. Accounts Receivable—Yes. I know I already wrote about A/R, but Accounts Receivable are so much worse for a law firm than most lawyers understand or appreciate. So much worse! And so, I'm going to say more about your A/R here. Because in the grand scheme of things, as important as your law firm's A/R is, I know it's about the ninth thing on your mind that you're going to want to (or be willing to) discuss with your bookkeeper each month.

Please Consider These Facts: A law firm incurs a cost to market, sell, produce, and deliver work to help its clients. To begin with, there are the marketing costs to acquire the client, like the salary for whoever meets with the prospective new client and converts them into someone who should be a paying client of the firm. Then there are the costs of the secretarial, paralegal, and associate time invested doing the work. In a well-run law firm, these labor costs are usually around 1/3 of total revenues. And that includes paying the owner at the same rate as an associate when you are wearing the hat of the associate and at the same rate you'd expect to pay a secretary when the owner is doing the job of a secretary. **For a more detailed explanation of how to calculate the "normalized salary" for the owner** of any given law firm based on how many hours they're wearing which "hat," please follow this link:

Let's say your law firm has a great client (Client A) who really relies on the firm, and your law firm delivers ten thousand dollars ($10,000)

worth of work. Except Client A doesn't pay their bill. Keep in mind, about $3,300 of that $10,000 already went out the door on salaries. Another $3,300 was likely spent on marketing, sales, rent, insurance, etc. Only $3,300 of the $10,000 is really "profit." Except the client owes you the full $10,000. They didn't say, "Well, I think I'll pay for your labor costs and for my share of the operating costs of the business, and I'll only stiff you on your profits." No, they stiffed you on the whole bill, which means the profits you'd normally enjoy from two other cases are now tied up in this one.

Client A received $10,000 of productive work from your law firm, which cost the firm $3,300 in labor and $3,300 in other costs related to running the business. But they didn't pay their bill, thereby denying you your $3,300 of profit.

Client B also gets $10,000 of productive work from the law firm but pays their bill. Keep in mind, the firm incurred another $3,300 in labor costs related to Client B's case or matter. And the firm will allocate the next $3,300 it receives from Client B to cover other costs of running the business related to Client B. But instead of going into the owner's pocket, guess where the last $3,300 from Client B's fee payment goes? That's right. It goes to cover the labor costs from Client A.

And now, guess where the money comes from to cover the firm's business expenses that should have been paid for out of revenues collected from Client A? Right again. It comes from money that the owners of the firm should have taken as profits from Client C.

And now, guess how much energy and enthusiasm the owner(s) of this law firm probably has left when they sit down to meet with Client D to talk about that prospective new client's important case or matter? Exactly.[20]

---

[20] The correct answer is: "not much." You wouldn't have much enthusiasm either if you just worked three cases and made zero profit.

So, about the ninth thing you probably want to talk about with your bookkeeper every month is the state of the firm's Accounts Receivable. But as you can see, this subject really deserves a place higher up on your list of priorities. Of course, in a well-run law firm, there is really no reason to have any Accounts Receivable at all, not if you're using the IOLTA client property trust account the way it was MEANT to be used.[21]

But we all make mistakes. And we all let things slide sometimes. So, we all wind up with some A/R from time to time. And now that you appreciate just how UNPROFITABLE A/R is for your law firm, you'll understand why I say that a bookkeeper who doesn't zero in on this with you each month truly, truly sucks.

What you want from your bookkeeper is a report each month showing not only the total amount of A/R but also broken down into tranches by age. Because obviously, the costs to you of not having it increase and the chances of ever collecting money owed to you declines with age. So, we want to see all the A/R that's been owed between:

0-30 DAYS:	**$X**
31-60 DAYS:	**$X**
61-90 DAYS:	**$X**
OVER 90 DAYS:	**$X**

Okay, what I just wrote above is pretty basic. And if your bookkeeper isn't at least giving you an Aged A/R Report, please fire that bookkeeper

---

21 To watch a very simple lesson on how to **use your law firm's IOLTA Client Property Trust Account as the profitable tool it was MEANT to be,** please go here:

immediately. I'm serious. That's an immediate firing offense and demonstrates a shocking level of incompetence. Sadly, it no longer shocks me whenever I meet the owner of a law firm who is struggling, and they have no idea about the state of their firm's A/R.

ATTENTION CONTINGENCY LAWYERS:

Instead of seeing an Aged A/R Report, you should see an Aged Case Cost Report. What costs have you sunk into each case and for how long? And while we're on the subject, I also want you to group your cases together based on which quarter you reasonably expect to collect how much revenue from each case. This way, you can project cash flow instead of going around sounding like a moron who says,

"I have a contingency law firm, therefore I cannot project revenues, expenses, or profits, duuhhh please pass the salami."

A better bookkeeper will not only present the Aged A/R Report to you, but they'll also include columns under each tranche with the name and contact information of the client and the name of the attorney in your law firm who is giving away all of your profits. What you want to look out for isn't just that "Client X owed us $5,000 last month." When you have a better bookkeeper, they'll present a report showing the "movement" of Client X's A/R. This way, you can see it happening when last month, Client X had $5,000 in arrears for 60 days, and this month, the same Client X now has the same $5,000 in arrears but for 90+ days . . . and wait for it . . . how did this happen? They also have a fresh new $2,500 in arrears for 30 days!

This means SOMEONE IN YOUR OFFICE IS STEALING FROM YOU.

They may not be stealing money and putting it into their own pocket. But they're stealing time. They're giving away work for free. Nay! They're allowing you to advance labor costs and other business operating costs so they can do work for free and keep doing more work for free. And 99% of the time when you dig into this sort of thing, what you're going to find is that your attorneys are getting their self-esteem from the clients, and from praise. Your attorneys may even be fooling themselves into believing that by allowing you to continue paying them and the rest of the staff and the rent and the insurance and everything else while the firm works for free, they're somehow building or protecting a relationship with a good client.

Let me ask you three potentially painful questions:

1. Whose relationship do you think that attorney is trying to build or protect when they take the pay you give them and do work for the client for free?

2. What's "good" about a client who doesn't pay their own bill and asks you to suck profits from other cases or matters to subsidize their own?

3. Do you really think that clients of your law firm appreciate you for not being willing or able to stand up for yourself to ensure

you get paid what you are owed, or do you think that maybe (just "maybe") they think that you are a fool and that they are actually losing respect for you because they know you'll **work for compliments instead of cash?**

And so it is with Accounts Receivable. There's just nothing good about them.

CHAPTER 15

A MUCH DEEPER DIVE INTO THE DRIVERS OF PROFIT THAN MOST STRUGGLING LAW FIRM OWNERS ARE EVER WILLING TO TAKE

10. Open/Close Case Ratio—Okay, here's something you don't need to understand, but you do need to know about it to make your life a lot better and also to help you better understand and appreciate why your bookkeeper may be falling so short of the standards I want you to keep for a bookkeeper.

Sixty percent of the cases your firm will handle have probably been pretty similar. Similar fact patterns. Similar amount of prep work. Similar outcomes. Twenty percent probably went off the rails. And twenty percent went much better than usual. How do I know this? Because I've worked with tens of thousands of law firms since 1999.

The point is that the majority of the cases your firm has ever handled and the majority of the cases your firm will likely ever handle are very similar from a business-operations standpoint.

Every practice area and every case type, or category of case or matter within a given case type, is different, of course. But within any given case type, there's usually a very narrow range of variance(s) in terms of the number of attorney hours, paralegal hours, and other case costs required

139

of a well-managed law firm to handle a given case type—regardless of how the firm bills for the work.

Okay, let's say that you are working with an experienced law firm Business Management Advisor, or you employ a full-time Professional Legal Administrator and/or CFO. And so, you study all of this. And you crunch the numbers. And you figure out that in your law firm the ratio is 1:100. In other words, one attorney can keep up with 100 active cases at a time. It doesn't matter for the purposes of this example if the ratio in your law firm is higher or lower. We're going to use 1:100 to keep the math simple.

So, your firm has one associate. And for the purposes of our example, we're going to say that we've studied your firm's systems and determine that in your law firm, one associate working in concert with related support staff can stay on top of about 100 active cases.

In other words, if they were "fully loaded," they'd have 100 open and active cases or matters. Except you never want to run your staff at exactly 100% full capacity in a small law firm. Or else you risk burnout, and the smaller the law firm, the less margin for error you have. So, let's say you decide you want to run the firm at 80% full capacity. That would be 80 cases, right?

(Yes, because 80% of 100 is 80.)

Now, we decide we want to get serious about strategically growing the business. So, we begin tracking how many new cases or matters are opened each month vs. how many cases or matters are closed each month. If the open vs. close rate is the same, then the firm will always have 80 open and active cases. Start with 80 cases. Open 10 new cases. Close 10 old cases. End with 80. Makes sense, yes?

(Yes, this makes sense.)

But what happens if marketing begins to outpace production, and now we're opening 15 cases but still the firm's means of production can only close 10 cases per month. In the first month when this happens, you'll probably be pretty happy! Start with 80 cases. Open 15 new cases.

Close 10 old cases. End with 85. Now we're at 85% capacity. We'll soon have a bit of extra revenue floating around!

Now consider what happens next month because you decided NOT to sabotage a marketing machine that's beginning to work. Next month, the firm will start with 85 cases. It will open 15 new cases. Close 10 old cases. End with 90. Cash flow is great. And you are happy. And your staff is busy. But not yet burning out. Life is good.

So, you keep your foot on the accelerator. And in month three, we start with 90 cases. Open 15 new cases. Close 10 old cases. End with 95. Wow, things are really beginning to get exciting!

If you keep up this pace, the firm goes from a very relaxed and sustainable 80% capacity to 100% full capacity in four months. If the firm has enough associates and enough support staff and a robust-enough recruiting, onboarding, and training program, and plenty of working capital to jump-start new staff, this may not be a problem. Because with 20 associates (for example), if one quits or must be terminated, or if someone gets sick, takes maternity/paternity leave for three months, etc., we can spread the work around and everyone can just run harder for awhile. But in a small law firm with only two lawyers, if one goes down, their full caseload lands on top of the other, which is obviously not sustainable.

Until now, we've only been talking about cases and lawyers. But there are paralegal ratios, secretarial ratios, and issues of physical plant and implications as to working capital, etc., etc. And remember, I told you that you don't have to understand any of this. You just have to know about it. Because the point is that in a well-managed law firm, these ratios are identified, understood, and managed ahead of time. And your bookkeeper who does not suck will present these open vs. closed reports to management each month to help you make preemptive moves. This way, you can be proactive instead of reactive in your decision-making, which is a much better way for you to live your life.

11. Average Case Value—Okay, now we're getting into some areas of discussion normally reserved for owners of eight-figure law firms and, of course, with any given Member of How To Manage A Small Law Firm, too. Just as we said, around 60% of any given case type will require (about) the same amount of labor—similarly, about 60% of any given case type your firm regularly handles will produce about the same amount of revenues and profits for your law firm.

It doesn't matter if your firm bills by the hour, if you've embraced flat fees, or if yours is a contingency firm. In fact, I would go so far as to say that it would be somewhat reckless and irresponsible to offer flat fees or monthly retainers, advance case costs, and/or make your fee contingent upon the outcome of a case until and unless you have a solid handle on the average case value. And the average case costs vary per case type, especially if you're the one advancing the costs![22]

I've worked with tens of thousands of solo and small law firm owners (and plenty of not-so-small law firm owners) since 1999.

When pushed to "guess," almost everyone can come pretty close to figuring out their firm's average case or matter value (ACV). An easy way to figure out your firm's ACV is to simply divide total gross revenues collected by the total number of cases or matters the firm closed last year. No matter if you like or dislike the number, that's still going to be the ACV of your law firm

($100,000/100 cases = $1,000 ACV).

A bookkeeper who doesn't suck will help you track this number so you can see if your law firm's ACV is trending up or down—preferably

---

22 ATTENTION CONTINGENCY LAW FIRM OWNERS: It is very easy to **predict, manage and even-out cash flow in a contingency practice.** Very, very easy. In fact, it's easier to do this in a contingency practice than with almost any other billing method. Hint, hint:

in time to get ahead of it and solve the problem if it's headed in the wrong direction, or, better yet, in time to get ahead of it and capitalize on it (with more marketing, probably) if it's headed in the right direction! Especially if you notice the ACV is growing for a particular case or matter type, from a particular marketing channel, or when entrusted to a particular paralegal, for example.

BONUS: Another very important concept that will have a very big impact on profits and your sanity is called "Cost Of Goods Sold" (COGS). A bookkeeper who does not suck should be able to help you calculate your law firm's COGS. For a very good explanation that even a child can understand about **what COGS is and why COGS are so important**, please follow this link:

12. Average Case Calendar Time (ACCT)—Remember way back in the beginning of this chapter when we talked about the timing of revenues being important? Well, related to Average Case Value, we also want to track the ACCT. This is very different from knowing how many "billable hours" goes into the average case or matter. That's "clock time."

Tracking ACCT gives us insight into how fast cash flows through a law firm. If we can shorten the average case calendar time, it will go a long way toward smoothing out cash flow. That's because law firms that have long case calendar times require more and more working capital to keep things afloat, especially as the firm grows.

Imagine two law firms handling the exact same type of cases, with the exact same cost of goods sold and the exact same profit margins. Except Firm A opens, closes, and gets paid for a case in an average of 90 days, as compared to Firm B that doesn't see the profits from a case and must float the costs (salaries, rent, etc.) for 180 days. That extra 90 days of "float" must be covered by what's called "working capital."

Let's say both law firms in our example gross $1.2 million. And to keep things simple, let's say they both collect exactly $100,000 per month.

How much working capital does Law Firm A need to always keep on hand? The answer is $300,000 because they must wait 90 days (3 months) until they can get paid. And so, the law firm has to "float" the case costs for 3 months x $100,000/month = $300,000.

How much working capital does Law Firm B need to always keep on hand? The answer is $600,000 because they must wait 180 days (6 months) until they can get paid, and so the law firm has to "float" the case costs for 6 months x $100,000/month = $600,000.

But wait, it gets worse! There's a cost to that working capital. Either it's being provided by a traditional lender who is likely charging interest, or it's being provided by your family in the form of money you could otherwise take out of your law firm and use to pay down your mortgage. Let's say the traditional lender charges 5% interest. And just to keep things simple, let's say your home mortgage is also 5%. That "extra" $300,000 is costing you $15,000 per year! Plus, wouldn't you prefer to have the extra equity in your home instead of "letting it ride" in your business?

So, for obvious reasons, we want to see the ACCT shrinking. Not at the expense of ACV, of course. It's a balancing act. It's a balancing act best performed with the help of an experienced law firm Business Management Advisor working in concert with a bookkeeper who doesn't suck to provide the reports needed to spot, monitor, and make smart strategic decisions.

13. Cost to Acquire a Client (CAC)—I've already explained several ways that a good bookkeeper can help you make your law firm more profitable. Now, let's talk about marketing!

A good bookkeeper will prepare and present reports to you and your business management advisors each month, which help you monitor marketing costs overall and ideally by marketing vendor or marketing channel. This, of course, assumes that your marketing vendors don't totally suck, which most of them do.

It may seem as if your law firm's marketing vendors are allergic to the idea of being held accountable for anything, which is why so many small law firm marketing vendors avoid building any means of tracking actual results into any of their marketing activities that they do for your law firm.

Unless, of course, they are just so stupid that they don't know why or how to build attribution tracking into the marketing they do for your law firm.

If that is the case, then why do they have such great tracking, accountability, and attribution measurements built into the marketing they do for themselves?!?!

Unless they don't even track their own marketing costs by channel? (What do you think?)

Either way, I'll leave it to you to decide which is worse: a marketing vendor who knows better but doesn't do better, or a marketing vendor who would do better if they knew better, but they don't!

Anyway, CAC is important because, unless you're tracking it, your CAC can get out of control in a hurry. And pretty soon, you'll wake up to find you're working for your marketing vendors instead of your marketing vendors working for you!

By the way, if you think I dislike bookkeepers who suck and you are excited about how much you've learned that will make your law firm more profitable and bring more sanity into your life by reading this book, then you should **read or listen to the audio of another book I wrote** to better understand why I dislike most small law firm marketing agencies so much more.

14. Labor Cost Ratio—Let me ask you a few pesky questions that may upset you, especially if your bookkeeper has never brought this up with you before:

Pesky Question #1: All things being equal, would you prefer that your law firm incur $300,000 in total labor costs to produce $1MM in revenue; or would you prefer that your law firm incur $400,000 in total labor costs to produce that same $1MM in revenue?

(Obviously, I'd prefer to operate my law firm more efficiently and have a 30% labor cost instead of a 40% labor cost because that extra $100,000 could pay for my kid's education.)

Pesky Question #2: Would you prefer that your law firm incur $300,000 in total labor costs to produce $1MM in revenue; or would you prefer that your law firm incur $400,000 in total labor costs to produce $1.3MM in revenue?

(All things being equal, if I can keep my labor costs to 30%, I'd prefer to invest the extra $100,000 on labor costs and generate an extra $300,000 in revenues because then I'd be able to take home about an extra $200,000 to educate two of my children.)

Pesky Question #3: Has your bookkeeper ever presented a Labor Cost Ratio and Trend Report to you to help you see if your firm's labor costs are outpacing gross revenues? And/or to empower you to make a proactive, strategic and intentional decision to front-load some labor costs for a few months to prepare your firm ahead-of-time "just in case" all those marketing plans you've made actually pan out?

Your bookkeeper should not presume to tell you what to do. That's an example of strategic advice best left to a CFO and/or Professional Legal Administrator based on your overall goals for your business and your life. But your bookkeeper ought to at least be bringing this information to your attention.

15. ROI Per Direct Revenue Producer—Andy Apple is great. You love Andy. Andy is the life of every party. Andy tells great stories about all of his most brilliant legal maneuvers. You like Betty. Betty Banana is nice. She is friendly and polite, always has a positive attitude, and is happy to share the credit for her legal victories with the whole staff who supported her in the case. Carl Cantalope is nice enough. You like working with Carl. But you don't think of him as a friend. You rarely invite Carl to lunch, and when he sees you and Andy leaving the office and tags along, you don't mind. But you're really looking forward to hearing Andy's next hilarious story.

Andy's salary is $100,000 per year. Betty's salary is $90,000 per year. And when Carl came to work, he asked for, and you agreed to, a salary of $80,000. But lately, they've all been asking you for a raise. And it's a competitive market, so you know they have other options. Fortunately, you've recently begun working with a bookkeeper who does not suck. And in your first monthly meeting, you are presented with a report showing ROI by Direct Revenue Producer.

It turns out that Andy's ROI for all of last year was 2:1, Betty's ROI was 3:1, and Carl's ROI was 4:1. That means Andy produced $200,000 of gross revenue for the firm; Betty produced $270,000; and Carl, beautiful, profitable Carl, produced $320,000 for the firm.

In other words, after paying related non-labor overhead expenses (office space, IT support, and other expenses that must be "spread out" across all your direct revenue producers), you either broke even or maybe you even lost some money on your friend Andy. The firm earned about $90,000 profit from its employment of Betty. And Carl's work is responsible for upwards of $160,000 of your law firm's profits.[23]

Put another way, at these rates of production, if you brought them each up to the same salary of, let's just say, $100,000 and didn't change anything else, Carl would still be responsible for around $140,000 of

---

23 This assumes the law firm in question operates anywhere close to "The Rule of Thirds" whereby about 1/3 of every dollar a lawyer generates gets split three ways: Labor Costs directly related to the work; General Overhead (rent, utilities, insurance, marketing costs, etc.); and Shareholder Profits. Keep in mind, the faster your law firm is growing, the more aggressively you'll likely have to invest in future capacity which will tend to throw off this "rule of thumb" ratio.

shareholder profit; the firm's employment of Betty would still produce a respectable $80,000 ROI; and you'd still be just breaking even on Andy and more likely losing some money around the edges. Now, how do you like them apples?

(No, this whole example was not just an excuse to say that! ☺)

16. Core Working Capital—Imagine a law firm with exactly one million two hundred thousand dollars ($1,200,000) of annual revenue. And imagine if the owner of this law firm were to meet a magical fairy who provided some magic fairy dust, which caused the law firm to experience perfectly aligned monthly income and expenses. And imagine, too, if said owner of said law firm didn't just "mean to get around to" sprinkling said magic fairy dust around the office but instead acted on said sprinkling intentions.

Then every month, exactly $100,000 of revenue would come in as revenue, and exactly $100,000 would go out in the form of expenses, including owner salary, benefits, etc.

So, in January, $100,000 would come in, and in January, $100,000 would go out.

In February, $100,000 would come in, and in February, $100,000 would go out.

Everything would be in perfect balance. And life would be simple. It would feel just like having a job where someone else takes responsibility for being the business owner.

But then one day, the magical fairy decided to go on vacation. And the supply of magic fairy dust soon ran out. So, in the next month, only $99,000 of revenue came in. Oh no, $100,000 worth of expenses must still go out! What are we going to do?

At this point, all the owner's big plans and grand ideas are going to have to be set aside because the owner's focus must be reduced to a singular and relatively small goal: "I must find $1,000."

This makes the owner of the law firm unhappy.

But imagine if the firm had just $10,000 of "core working capital" on hand to act as a cushion for the inevitable ups and downs that occur in the real world. Then, when $99,000 of revenue comes in, the owner can stay focused on the bigger picture and wait 30 days to see if $101,000 comes in next month. Or maybe $102,000 comes in the month after that. The point is that with some "cushion," we can stay focused on what we need to stay focused on instead of allowing temporary cash flow variances to distract us from our plans.

Most people will tell you that two months of core working capital is ideal to smooth out cash flow. When I launched How To Manage A Small Law Firm in 2009, I was flat-out broke with no credit, and I had days, not months or even weeks, of core working capital. It was very stressful. And it was difficult to think or prioritize long-term growth initiatives, which was very frustrating.

Nowadays, How To Manage Enterprises—which owns How To Manage A Small Law Firm and Small Law Firm Bookkeeping That Does Not Suck—grosses more than $3MM per month as of this writing. And we have not only two months core working capital on hand, but also a healthy line of credit, too. So let me tell you, as someone who has experienced both ends of the spectrum, life is MUCH easier when you have some cushion. Plus, it's a lot more fun to run your business this way because you can do so on YOUR terms.

But you'd be mistaken if you believed that the reason life is so much easier "this way" is because of the dollar amounts involved. There are plenty of firms much larger than How To Manage with far fewer days of core working capital on hand and little access to credit. For the owners of those firms, life is still very stressful. And they're usually still frustrated daily by the need to postpone long-range plans to chase short-term cash flow. So please, don't put this important subject out of your mind, thinking that one day, you'll outgrow it because you will not live it down. And so, when a problem comes along with your law firm's core working capital, you must whip it.[24]

Keep in mind that the average small law firm in the United States grows top-line gross revenue at an average rate of right around 5% year-over-year. At this modest rate of growth, a 15% profit margin is usually more than enough to fund core working capital. And the owners of those law firms can afford to be "sloppy" when it comes to core working capital.

But you'd be hard pressed to find many law firms managed by How To Manage A Small Law Firm that are growing at LESS THAN 30%-50% year-over-year, which means we have a lot of experience paying close attention to core working capital because the law firms we manage are constantly outgrowing their core working capital. By choice.

Here's how it works: A well-managed small law firm with relatively "flat" growth ought to produce around 20% profit on net income (net operating income or "NOI"). In other words, a $1MM law firm ought to produce around $200,000 NOI.

So, that $1MM law firm with a two month "cushion" of monthly working capital has about $160,000 in working capital. Next year, it grows by just 5% from $1,000,000 to $1,050,000. And profits grow from $200,000 to $210,000. To maintain the firm's two month "cushion," the owners agree to allow the business to retain $8,000 from their profit earnings. In other words, the owners could have taken the full $10,000 (20% of the extra $50,000), but instead, they chose to protect their two-month cushion and took only an additional $2,000 in profits out of the business.

---

24 Whip it good. Follow this link to see a more detailed lesson about **the relationship between Core Working Capital and your sanity.** It's not too late.

Now, consider what happens when the owners decide to embark on a strategy of rapid growth. Let's say we're going to dial up growth from 5% to 25%. Instead of an additional $50,000 of gross revenue, we should expect an extra $250,000. Except, to prepare for this growth, we had to hire another paralegal and provide that person with all the equipment and training needed to set them up for success. Plus, there was a recruiting fee. And that $250,000 of additional revenue didn't just appear by magic because we used some cool buzzwords (like "dialing up growth"). There were actual marketing expenses behind those results, and not everything we did to "dial up growth" worked perfectly the first time because the growth happened out here in the real world.

So, overall expenses went up, and profit margins probably went down from 20% to, let's say, 10%, which means that $160,000 of working capital now only represents a month and a half of "cushion," not two whole months. And instead of making $200,000 on $1MM, this year, we're looking at making $125,000 on $1.25MM.

"Okay, RJon, but what if my law firm isn't a seven-figure law firm? What if my firm is only grossing $125,000 per year, not $1.25 million dollars per year? Does this still apply to me?"

Yes, it does! Please re-read what I just wrote above. Just remove a digit from the example and it will work exactly the same for you.

Here's my point: The chances are slim that you will ever be able to grow your $125,000 law firm into a $1MM, $500,000, or even $250,000 law firm without having to navigate these issues. And the chances that you will be able to navigate these issues successfully and without inflicting great damage on yourself, without the benefit of solid financial reports to use as your map, are even more slim. This is precisely why most struggling law firms never outgrow the miserable revenue range between $0 to around $250,000 when everything is so much harder on the owner of the firm. Yes! It does get easier. Running a $1MM law firm is easier than running a $500,000 law firm. Just as running a $500,000 law firm is easier than running a $250,000 law firm. Just as running a $2MM law firm is so much easier than a $1MM law firm. Actually, it's right around $1.5MM (in 2023 dollars) when things really become so much easier.[25]

Your chances are going to be greatly enhanced as soon as you begin to pay attention to how your firm is using its core working capital. And, if the point is not already clear, your bookkeeper who does not suck ought to be putting a report in front of you every month to show you visually how the firm is using its core working capital and whether and how quickly it's outgrowing its core working capital. This way, you and your small law firm's business management advisors can make informed, proactive, and strategic decisions about whether, when, and how aggressively to grow the firm.

The more your firm grows, the more people it can help. Or put another way, the only way for your law firm to grow is to help more people. Either way, if you believe you have a gift, then I sincerely hope you will grow your law firm so you can share your gift with more people!

■ ■ ■

---

25 Follow this link to see a fuller **explanation about the seven stages of a law firm's growth** so you can know what to expect:

CHAPTER 16

AND NOW LET'S TALK ABOUT WHAT YOUR BOOKKEEPER NEEDS...

Here's *what most bookkeepers do.* They begin by asking you all the questions and discussing all the issues that are important to them, which makes their job easier. Then, they run out of time and never get around to any of the topics or issues discussed throughout the second part of this book. Which are all the topics that matter the most to you and make your job easier.

Until now, I've been pretty rough on sucky bookkeepers. But really, I'm a big fan of bookkeepers. It's only the ones who suck that I hope you've understood me to be referring to in my critique. A good book-keeper is a great asset to any entrepreneur. They give you the infor-mation you need to build a better law firm, which helps more people and makes the world a better place for all of us. Try building a hugely successful law firm that can do massive good in this world without the business being profitable. You can't do it. So now, I need to say a few words about sucky clients.

Have you ever had a legal client who was uncommunicative? Someone who is difficult to schedule appointments with and who doesn't always show up on time or even at all? Someone who, when they do show up,

153

seems like their mind is somewhere else and not on the matter at hand—almost as if they've mentally decided it's "your" case and not their case?

How about the legal client who expects you to "just know" things that you could not possibly know unless they have the patience to sit and answer your legitimate questions—which, as I've already described, they don't—and yet when things go wrong, they take zero responsibility for their lack of participation, cooperation, and/or communication?

Have you ever had a legal client like that?

And speaking of when things go wrong, have you ever had a legal client who gets so distracted by the minutiae of a case that they miss the bigger picture? Or how about that client who feels out of control and tries to satisfy their need to feel in control by nitpicking a million little details that really don't matter: "I was reviewing your draft Motion for Summary Judgment and I noticed the following minor details aren't exactly the way I'd have said them, plus there's a comma out of place on page 5." As if the judge is going to decide the MSJ one way or the other depending on whether the parties first met six years ago or six and a half years ago and/or based on punctuation.

Have you ever had a legal client like that? Do you really need me to tell you not to be a bookkeeping client like that? You probably do not need me to remind you that despite your best efforts as their lawyer, we all know clients like that never get the best out of their lawyer and, consequently, they never get the best results.

Don't be that sort of bookkeeping client. Don't be the sort of person who expects your bookkeeper to use their non-existent powers of mental telepathy to know that lunch you paid for with John Doe on the firm's credit card is a marketing expense (for example) and not a personal expense.

And it is not the sign of a "bad" bookkeeper if your books balance, the reports delivered to you provide actionable insight about your business, and your bookkeeper even takes the time to walk you through everything; but some minor expenses are mis-categorized in the draft, which can be easily corrected in the final books for the month or with a simple "recasting" of the books for the month IF it turns out that expense from the office supply store for a box of pencils (instead of pens) really makes a difference in the grand scheme of things.

Remember, the purpose of bookkeeping is to give you a historical record with which to understand what has happened in your business and to give your financial accountant the information required to accurately report income and expenses of the firm. The IRS does not care about the categories of those expenses. And so, you should only care about the categories of those expenses to the extent that they help inform your management decisions on a going-forward basis.

So, your bookkeeper—even if you could find the world's best book-keeper—is going to need input and answers from you. Otherwise, they'll just have to guess. And most of their guesses will probably be wrong because they're just guessing. And then, your law firm's financials will be garbage. And then, the decisions you make based on the finan-cials of your business will be garbage. And then, you will either lose or lose out on the opportunity to make your law firm a lot more profit-able—without you having to do a whole bunch of extra work, just a couple of very profitable, admittedly unglamorous, entrepreneurial hours a month.

Please do not interpret the fact that I left this discussion until the end of this book to mean that this is the least impor-tant part of the conversation. This is a critical part of the conversation. Without this part of the conversation, the rest of the discussions would not be possible. It's just that too many bookkeepers and too many of their clients who don't know any better feel satisfied that they have done their job by ONLY having this last part of the conversation. Whereas from my perspective

*This is a **critical** part of the conversation.*

as an entrepreneur with several seven- and eight-figure businesses—
and hopefully by now you agree with me—the whole point of this
last part of the conversation is to make it possible to have the rest of
the discussion.

I know what you are thinking right now. What you are thinking is:
"Holy crap, RJon, could you possibly be more dramatic?" What are you
talking about!?!? The answer is yes. I could be more dramatic if I really
wanted to be. But I don't. So, here's what I'm talking about:

GARBAGE IN = GARBAGE OUT

It is important that your bookkeeper gets timely answers to the
questions they'll inevitably have so they can put revenues and expenses
in the correct categories. This way, revenues and expenses can be
properly attributed. Otherwise, when you sit down to conduct your
analysis and make your strategic planning decisions, you're liable to
get unprofitable results because you may be making good decisions,
but those decisions are based on inaccurate information, so the results
won't make you happy.

Remember, your bookkeeper is a bookkeeper, not a mind reader.
It is the height of entrepreneurial immaturity for a law firm owner
to criticize a bookkeeper for "not knowing" what it is nearly impossible for a bookkeeper to know without speaking with the owner of
the business.

For example, how is even the world's best bookkeeper supposed to
know whether the expense that appears on your credit card as "Kramerica
Industries, Incorporated" is a business or a personal expense? And even
if your bookkeeper can figure out that it's a business expense, without
speaking with you, how are they supposed to know whether it's:

- A Marketing Expense—because you took a referral source to lunch at Kramerica's restaurant, which only serves PB&J sandwiches; or

- A Sales Expense—because you decided that it would improve sales if you wore a new cologne or perfume called "The Beach" when meeting with prospective new clients; or

- Should that credit card expense factor into the labor cost ratio because it was related to the employment of an intern named Darren?

- Without input from you, how is your bookkeeper supposed to know that credit card expense, which only appears as "Kramerica Industries, Inc.," should be categorized as an expense for the firm's physical plant because you purchased a coffee-table book about coffee tables that itself functions as a coffee table for the reception area of your law firm?

- And what about the expense for all that ketchup and mustard packaged together in the same bottle? Without your input, how is your firm's bookkeeper supposed to know that it should be categorized as an improvement to the processes and procedures by preventing staff from wasting valuable time handling two different containers of condiments during their lunch breaks?

And last but not least . . .

- Should that expense that appears on the law firm's credit card be categorized under "financial controls and risk management" because it was spent on an oil bladder system manufactured by Kramerica Industries, Incorporated?

The point is that if you want your firm's financial reports to mean anything, you are going to have to be patient and suffer through some probably tedious questions each month that even the world's best book-keeper will still need to ask you in order to make sure all the revenues and expenses are put into the proper categories.

I hope by now I have earned your trust enough to say: "Believe me, it will be worth it." Because it will!

Oh, and one more thing: Whether you are working with my own bookkeeping company or any other bookkeeper, please do not go out of your way to avoid seeing the forest because you're obsessed with a few leaves being in the wrong categories each month.

It's probably not such a big deal.

The correct response when (not if) minor mistakes are discovered in some (likely most) months is to ask the following three questions:

1. Is it material? Does it change my analysis or understanding of the overall financial performance of my business if the expense for paperclips was miscategorized as being an expense for staples? If not, then zoom out. See the big picture and accept your book-keeper's assurance that the categorization will be corrected in next month's financials.

2. If it DOES make a material difference, then you have a mature decision to make: "Is this important enough to derail the rest of my analysis today, or can I just sort of factor this into my think-ing and ask my bookkeeper to 'recast' this month's financials and send me the revised financials tomorrow?"; and finally

3. Gee, I wonder if maybe there's something of more significance I'm trying to avoid looking at, seeing, or dealing with, and maybe (just maybe) that is why I am trying to make this whole meeting

all about a relatively minor error or mis-categorization, which can be easily corrected and incorporated into a revised set of "recast" financials along with a simple note of explanation from the bookkeeper:

"Financials for the month of X recast to reflect correct categorization of ABC as this instead of that, based on monthly review with the owner of the law firm."

You see? No big deal.

■ ■ ■

CONCLUSION

Thank you for reading this book, unless you just skipped to the end without reading everything I invested my time to write in an effort to help you. In which case, I'll save my thanks until you go back and read the book to earn your right to read these words. Or you might consider simply **listening to the audio version of this book**, which I've narrated for you myself.

Either way, thank you. At the beginning of this book, I told you that reading a book like this would probably piss you off. Hopefully, by now, you understand that wasn't my intention, but it was necessary—at least for most readers—to "break the spell" that seems to have fallen over so many struggling law firm owners.

I told you this book is meant to be a rallying cry for entrepreneurially minded small law firm owners everywhere and that it is dedicated to you if you are committed to finding a better way to grow your business and a better way to live your life.

If you implement what's explained in this book, your law firm will *definitely* become more profitable. You will feel more confidence. And you will begin to experience the unique satisfaction that comes from being able to reliably put more of the revenue collected by your law firm into your own personal bank account every month and quarter.

Those were my promises to you as author to reader. And I stand by them. No hedge words. If you implement anything I have shared with you throughout this book, you WILL begin to see some positive results in your business. If you implement a bit more, then pretty soon, more positive results will begin to show up for you. But this is not what most people will do. Sadly, what most people will do is read a book like this. They'll nod their heads. They'll make a bunch of notes in the margins. And then, they'll go out in search of an easier way in another book. What I want you to do instead is re-read this book. Or re-listen to the audio. Or if you're reading it now, then listen to it next time through. My point is that I want you to internalize the lessons, then I want you to take action so that you can experience the results. I didn't agree to write this book to teach anyone anything; I wrote it to help people get results!

One of the side effects of internalizing and acting upon the lessons in a book like this is that you may also begin to feel more lonely because it truly is lonely at the top. Most small law firm owners would prefer (as evidenced by their actions) to adapt themselves to unpleasant circumstances than take unusual actions that may subject them to unflattering judgments, comments, and the petty criticisms of others. But what else other than "something different than everyone else is doing" can possibly produce effects that are so much better (and different) than what most small law firm owners have banded together and agreed upon as being "normal"?

So, if you are feeling a bit lonely on your entrepreneurial journey, I want to tell you that you are not actually alone. There are more than a thousand of us who get together in person several times throughout the year to learn, grow, celebrate one another's success, and share practical and highly profitable advice. Plus, there are many thousands more who get together online. Please visit www.ProfitFirstForLawyers.com or scan the QR code to **join our community**, and let's keep the conversation going.

ABOUT FEEDBACK

When *you speak out,* share videos, conduct workshops, or write a book like this—a book that challenges conventional wisdom—you expect to get a lot of feedback from readers. That feedback tends to fall into three main categories.

1. Messages of thanks from readers who share beautiful and heartfelt stories of law firms, clients, staff, and family who are all better off because they took what they learned and are implementing at least some of it.

2. Messages with questions from readers who need more information or with constructive suggestions for how to improve some aspect of the book or bonus materials.

3. And messages from readers who, as it often turns out, didn't actually read the whole book because they got "triggered" by something they read and wanted to write to tell you how wrong you are.

I welcome all comments, feedback, constructive criticism, and even not-so-constructive criticism. I have only one condition as to whether or not I'll bother to reply: You must tell me you have actually put at least some of my ideas to the test in the real world. I know from too much real-world experience with too many real lawyers in too many countless real law firms and in every practice area you can imagine that this stuff works. It just plain works. So please, don't waste my time (or yours) trying to tell me why you "think" that it won't.

Please share your feedback: Feedback@ProfitFirstForLawyers.com

Please share your success stories:
SuccessStories@ProfitFirstForLawyers.com

Please share your criticisms & insults:
Insults@ProfitFirstForLawyers.com

If you are a member of the press and you would like to book me or someone from my team for an interview, podcast, talk, talent show, or anything else that might be interesting, please use this email address: Press@ProfitFirstForLawyers.com

If you would like to know the personal telephone number or home address of Mike Michalowicz, I will not give it to you, but you can get in touch with his team at Support@ProfitFirstProfessionals.com.

■ ■ ■

PROFIT FIRST SUMMARY

When *I was a kid* there were these book summaries called CliffsNotes™. They were no substitute for actually reading the book, but they'd get you through an exam by summarizing the highlights. In case "somehow" you managed to forget to read the book. Anyway, CliffsNotes™ is a registered trademark so what follows is NOT the CliffsNotes™ version of *Profit First* by Mike Michalowicz—just my notes ☺.

As I've said, you will get the most from this book by reading it along with the original *Profit First*, not instead of reading it. But in case you haven't gotten around to reading *Profit First* yet or maybe it's been awhile and you could use a little refresher, here are all the core principles.

Profit First shows you how to turn your business into a profit-breathing machine, first by rejecting traditional methods of cash management and accounting which obviously do not work for so many small businesses.

Most small business owners—

I was going to say "embrace" except that would suggest it is a conscious or intentional decision. So instead, I'll say most small business owners who don't know any better wind up settling for the following approach to profits:

1. Sell as much as they can sell.

2. Pay everyone else first.

3. Keep whatever is left over.

The problem is that the formula is backward.

PARKINSON'S LAW

In *Profit First* Mike talks about Parkinson's Law, which states that how long it will take to finish anything depends on how long you have to get it done. So if you have a month to get something done, it will take you a month to get it done. But if you have just three days to get the same thing done, "somehow" you will find a way to get it done in just three days.

The same works with money in business. If your business has $100 available in its cash operating account, you will find that you need all of it to operate the business; if the same business has just $90 in the cash operating account, you will find a way to operate the business on just $90. In fact, the business will be leaner, meaner and more innovative because you will be "forced" to become more creative and resourceful. And you'll also have $10 of profit!

GROWTH VS. PROFIT

Growth is only half the equation. It is an important half, but still only half.

THE PRIMACY EFFECT

In *Profit First*, Mike also tells us about how The Primacy Effect affects the profitability of our businesses. It states that you tend to pay more attention to what comes first and ignore everything else. This is why the "traditional" approach to cash management and profitability turns out to be so unprofitable. Because it puts profit last. Almost as an afterthought.

Instead, profit must be "baked in" to your business. Every day, every transaction, every moment. Profit cannot be treated as an event. It must be treated as a habit. But that is not how most business owners approach the profitability of their business. They try to grow their way out of their problems. As if the next big sale or customer or some angel investor is going to come along and save them. Which actually only makes things worse, because now those business owners are desperate. And anyone who is paying attention knows it.

A much healthier approach—a more rational approach—is to begin by deciding what you want to earn and take that out from your sales, first. After all, the business is supposed to be there to give you a better life, isn't it? Yes, this way of thinking about your relationship with your business may "force" you to make some tough decisions at work—or get creative. But it's better to be forced to make tough decisions at work than to have to make tough decisions at home.

PLATE SIZE AFFECTS CALORIE CONSUMPTION

When you sit down for dinner with a giant plate, you naturally fill it, right? Sure, we all do.

But then one day Mike tells us in *Profit First*, he realized that if he removed all the oversized plates from his home and replaced them with smaller dishes and bowls, his family naturally took smaller portions and became healthier.

Your business finances are the same way. By separating revenues into separate, smaller portions, your business will naturally embrace financial portion control, too. Mike acknowledges this isn't a "new" idea. In fact, he talks about how his grandmother used to separate out the family's income every payday into separate envelopes, each designated for its own purpose. Same idea here.

The Profit First methodology operates with five different bank accounts, though you can (and I do) use more than these five foundational accounts if you see the need in your business. The five foundational accounts in Profit First are:

1. Main Income—This is the main account into which all gross revenue first enters the business before being separated out on a percentage basis that you will decide upon ahead of time. This is how we ensure you take your profits first!

2. Profits—Begin with just 1%. Just one percent. If your business can operate with $100, it can operate with $99. You won't even miss 1% in your operating account, but it will do something almost magical for your mindset when you see your personal profit account beginning to grow!

3. Owner's Salary—You probably aren't a totally passive investor in your business. You probably have a job too, working "in" the business. You wouldn't ask or expect anyone else to work for your business for free, so your business shouldn't ask or expect you to work for free, either. Put another way, imagine if you were injured and could not work "in" the business for a few months. Would you just close down the business, or would you hire someone else to cover for you and do the job(s) you normally do? Hopefully that's a rhetorical question. Obviously, you'd hire someone (or several people) to do the job(s) you normally do for the business. How much would the business have to pay those people? That's how much the IRS would tell you the owner's "normalized" salary ought to be set at.

4. Taxes—Hopefully your business is using a professional payroll service of some kind that's already deducting taxes from your normalized salary. But what about the profits? A bookkeeper who does not totally suck will help you figure out how much taxes ought to be set aside to pay the taxes on every dollar of salary or profits the business pays to you. In other words, by the time the

money reaches your hands personally, it ought to be all yours, with taxes already paid!

5. Operating Expenses—Instead of taking home whatever is "left over" for your family and then having to "get creative" at home, those of us who embrace Profit First as a way of life "force" ourselves to get creative with the money we have left over in the account for operating expenses. Yes, sometimes this requires us to make tough choices in our business, but we believe it's better to make tough choices in business than to have to make tougher choices at home.

■ ■ ■

CASE STUDIES

James Banks
Washington Auto Law
Seattle, WA

We specialize in helping people who have been hurt in auto accidents to navigate the insurance claims process.

How many team members do you have?
We currently operate with five full-time employees, and then we outsource our chief marketing officer, our management accountant and our bookkeeper that doesn't suck.

What is your law firm grossing?
In 2022, my law firm grossed $1.2 million.

What are your results before and after working with RJon?
Since I started working with RJon eight months ago, my firm has grown over 100%!

What did you think about *Profit First for Lawyers?*
Profit First for Lawyers should be required reading for all owners of solo and small law firms. It really helps you understand what the traditional model for profit is, and why it isn't helpful. *Profit First for Lawyers* helps you to put profits first.

What were some of your biggest takeaways after reading *Profit First for Lawyers?*

The book teaches you to decide ahead of time what percentage of every dollar of revenue you're going to scoop off the top for yourself. Then you get creative and find ways to make your business perform with what's left over. This is genius because it forces you to run your law firm in a way that is both efficient and innovative.

The foundation for what you're doing with the Profit First model is flipping the traditional profit model on its head, by focusing on your gross revenues, taking your profit first, and then operating your law firm with what's left over.

How did reading this book make you look at your business differently?

Profit First for Lawyers helped me rethink my law firm. It's no longer a business that I work *for*, rather it's a business that works *for me*. You start running your law firm like a lean, mean, moneymaking machine that works for you so that you can live your best life based on the goals that you set for yourself financially, personally, and professionally.

What was your biggest takeaway after implementing Profit First?

One of the genius things about implementing Profit First accounting principles is that you're not having to create all new habits. The fact is most of us have checking accounts and you check your bank accounts when you get to the office in the morning. You see how much money is in there, and then run your law firm based on that number. With Profit First, you still do that, only you have five different accounts that you look at. You're not just operating your law firm from one big expense account; you have different buckets with different numbers. You still are doing what you normally do, only you're doing it now in a way that's much more profitable.

What advice do you have for another attorney considering Profit First?

I've been using the Profit First model for six months now. Every dollar that I generate into the firm, I take 15% off the top. No questions asked before I do anything else. The first thing that comes out is my profit. The advice I have for everyone else that's considering Profit First is to just take action. Start implementing the ideas and the strategies that you learn and reap the rewards.

Would you recommend this book to another law firm owner?

As an owner of a seven-figure small law firm myself, I highly recommend all law firm owners of all sizes read *Profit First for Lawyers*. You really want to run your law firm as efficiently as possible. That's what *Profit First for Lawyers* will teach you how to do.

Marie Drake
Drake Law Firm
GOLDEN, CO

We specialize in no-bullshit divorce.

How many team members do you have?
We have five people at our firm right now. I have a full-time office manager and a full-time associate attorney here at the law firm. I also have some remote staff including a full-time receptionist/intake coordinator who also does some marketing and a three-quarter time paralegal. But I'm excited that we will have to do some more hiring and keep working on our marketing as we head towards the seven-figure number.

What is your law firm grossing?
In 2022, the law firm grossed $558,000 and in 2023 we are on track to break seven figures.

Has your law firm grown since implementing Profit First?
I started using Profit First in 2020, but it was sort of half-assed. I've been implementing it more seriously since January 2023. Just a year ago, I would be thrilled with grossing $30,000 a month and now I'm consistently having $65,000-$70,000 months. So that's super exciting! It's a big difference. We're doing a lot to get to those numbers, but I just want to see it continue to grow and I know a big part of it has to do with Profit First.

Do you view your law firm differently after reading *Profit First for Lawyers?*
Reading this book helped me view my law firm differently because it reminded me that most American law firms grow at a rate of 5% to 7% a year. And my law firm has been growing at ten times that, very consistently.

I mean, we doubled in 2021, we grew by 58% in 2022, and we're on track to double again in 2023. So, it has shown me that something right is happening here if we have these kinds of growth rates compared to what the average American law firm has.

What was your biggest takeaway after reading *Profit First for Lawyers*?

I've been following Profit First for several years now with my law firm as it grows. And my biggest takeaway from *Profit First for Lawyers* is that I love how specific it is for the industry that I'm in. I'm an attorney and I'm an entrepreneur and I'm running my own law firm. And this is really helping me figure out a completely sort of sober, rational way to run a business and ensure that there's always going to be a measure of profit.

What convinced you to start using Profit First, and what benefits did you see?

I kept running into all these attorneys who were using it and it was really working well for them. So, I started to just believe that it could work for me too. In the beginning it was a little bit nerve wracking because I still had the same issues that I had before I started Profit First, but those issues won't be here next year because we will have built up the surplus.

I think the biggest benefit that I saw right away was just the feeling of having some peace of mind around running the law firm and knowing there are savings if we have some kind of cash flow crunch because everybody has cash crunches. But if we have one, it's just a little blip. It's not a big looming cliff we're going over.

What advice do you have for another attorney considering Profit First?

I would tell the lawyer who is just starting to implement this, to just do it, just take the action. Whatever your feelings are around setting aside profit first, just do it. It shouldn't be a line item at the end of your spreadsheet, it should be at the top! Take whatever percentage you decide. I started really small. I started at 2%. Just take it and set it aside. And do what *Profit First* recommends you do, which is to go to a different bank and open an account and do not link the accounts. This way it's not so accessible. And I think you're going to feel good. But you have to take action.

Would you recommend this book to another law firm owner?

I would recommend other law firm owners read *Profit First for Lawyers*. I also think the principles really apply to anyone in business, and are a good way to run your life personally, too. So, if you get a paycheck for $2,000, try to set aside $200, put it in a savings account to build for investments, retirement or just for a rainy day.

Mackenzie Sorich
View Ridge Family Law and Estate Planning
SEATTLE, WA

How many team members do you have?
I currently have 15 employees.

What is your law firm grossing?
My law firm is currently grossing 1.5 million per year.

Has your law firm grown since implementing Profit First?
I started using Profit First around March of 2022 and I have seen growth in my business since implementing these principles. It is a little bit awkward at first. But setting aside a little bit of profit every month and then gradually increasing that profit bank account percentage little by little every time I take a draw from the operating account, is resulting in greater profit for my family and for myself and for all the work that I've done to endeavor in this entrepreneurial journey.

What results did you see right away after implementing Profit First?
The early benefits of reading *Profit First* and *Profit First for Lawyers* is the mindset shift that I've experienced. They have helped me put into perspective how the work that I'm doing for my firm, the sacrifices that I'm making as an entrepreneur, the risks that I'm taking as an entrepreneur can all be quantified, and paid off by setting aside my profit first to compensate for those risks and achieve the rewards that I've set out to achieve for myself and my family.

How has Profit First impacted your life in a personal and professional way?

Profit First has impacted my life by running my law firm in a different way. It's helped me reframe the work that I do and made me realize that I don't need to be a slave to my law firm. I don't need to toil away. The work that I'm doing is valuable and it's worthy of my efforts to put away the profit first and save that for my family and my personal use.

Reading *Profit First for Lawyers* has helped me better understand that the law firm should really serve our family. For years I suffered for my business, worked long hours, longer than my staff and my vendors. And after reading this book, I've come to a whole new mindset about why I'm an entrepreneur and why the firm should help me further my goals for my family and myself.

What are some dreams and goals you have accomplished since using Profit First?

Some of the things I've been able to achieve by using Profit First principles are taking bigger and better vacations with my family. I've been able to take a little bit more time away from my business than I used to. And we've been able to enjoy adventures around the world as a result of putting aside money into the Profit First account. We went to Italy last year and this year we will be going to England and France.

After reading the book, did you feel more empowered as a business owner?

I do feel more empowered as a firm owner and entrepreneur after reading *Profit First for Lawyers*. I learned that there are a number of reports I can ask my bookkeeper to produce so I can see what's going on. I don't need to be a corporate executive or have a whole lot of accounting training. I just need these reports, and to be familiar with them, so I know what's going on in my firm financially.

What advice do you have for another attorney considering Profit First?

My advice, if you're looking into Profit First for the first time, is just do it. Jump in there. Read the book as quickly as you can. You can always come back to it for clarification, but the sooner you start, the sooner you're going to be on your way to protecting your profits. My advice to someone who has just started using Profit First is to just keep trying at it.

Would you recommend this book to another law firm owner?

I already recommend *Profit First for Lawyers* to all of my lawyer friends who run small practices. I'm so excited to share this with some of my colleagues so that we can talk about these concepts and further our understanding and our progress in the financial controls of our firm.

Todd Wesche
Vetus Legal LLC
BOSTON, MA

I help veterans, and their dependents and survivors obtain the U.S. Department of Veterans Affairs (VA) benefits they deserve.

How many team members do you have?
We have four employees currently. We just hired a fifth person to expand the staff and provide more capacity. And then by the end of the year, I'm expecting to have between 8 to 12 employees.

What is your law firm grossing?
In 2022, my law firm grossed $600,000 and we're on a run rate for $1.2 million this year.

Has your law firm grown since implementing Profit First?
Since implementing Profit First, revenues are skyrocketing! I've been able to grow the business in ways I actually didn't expect as a side effect of profit. I thought that Profit First would just be about making sure I got paid first, which it does, but it also makes sure you allocate for taxes and payroll and various other things. By doing this, the stress and pressure on me was lifted because I already knew where the money was going to come from and I knew that it had been allocated.

What were some of the benefits you saw from implmenting Profit First?
Profit First allowed me to dedicate resources—which included my time, my energy, and my attention—to marketing, to sales, to client development, to staff development, to implementing new technologies, to doing all those things I'd been wanting to do, but had been too burnt out to

do because I didn't feel like I was getting rewarded. I didn't feel like I was getting what I wanted out of the company personally, professionally and financially.

How long have you used Profit First and were there any pitfalls after implementing?

I started using Profit First around June of 2022. My biggest struggle with Profit First, after a small test with just the profit account, was the extra accounts for other things like taxes, payroll, etc. Ultimately, the payroll account was the hardest one because I run a contingency based firm. So, what I've done instead is pretend that my payroll account is effectively my reserve account. I just dump everything into reserves and then I will take the money out of reserves and put it into the payroll account to make sure that money is there and then we run payroll out of that account.

What convinced you to start using Profit First?

The principles in *Profit First* are life-changing in many respects. It's amazing how some very simple tools and very simple changes in the way you approach money, the way you approach your finances, the way you approach how you keep records of things, and the way you allocate your resources can make a *huge* difference in the way that you see the money on the other end.

What advice do you have for another attorney considering Profit First?

If you're looking at Profit First for the very first time, don't get caught in the minutia. Think about it from the big picture of how this will help you. You might need to read the book(s) a couple of times. You might need to go through the process a couple of times before realizing how simple it actually is. Trust the simplicity of it, because simplicity is also what makes it doable.

Would you recommend this book to another law firm owner?

I would recommend both *Profit First for Lawyers* and *Profit First*, the original book. The simple reality is that the tools that these books teach are very simple to implement, but they are extraordinarily powerful because of the way they teach you how to think about money and your own entitlement to that money.

Andy Wyman
Wyman Legal Solutions
Boca Raton, FL

We provide legal Services for construction, business, and property damage issues.

How many team members do you have?
At the moment, we have two lawyers, a paralegal, a legal assistant and an executive assistant. In total we have six employees right now (including myself).

What is your law firm grossing?
In 2022, my law firm grossed $1,135,000. Through the first quarter of 2023, we grossed 440,000, so we're on pace for about $1,750,000.

What are your results before and after working with RJon?
Since I started working with RJon, my law firm's revenues have grown from about 180,000 to where I am now, which is almost 10x growth of my law firm since the end of 2018.

What did you think about *Profit First for Lawyers?*
Profit First for Lawyers was an excellent read. It was super informative, not only on the Profit First methods and the systems that we can employ to set aside money for the things that we're going to need in the future; but it was also an interesting look at some of the financial metrics that we should really be considering and looking at as business owners.

What was your biggest takeaway after reading *Profit First for Lawyers*?

There is a chapter in *Profit First for Lawyers* that talks specifically about the different types of things that you want to consider putting money aside for: not just your profit as the owner of the business, but for specific types of expenses and categories of expenses like marketing expenses, maybe for raises or bonuses for your staff, and even for things you want to try to achieve in the future like real estate investments or other purchases like that.

What are some dreams and goals you have accomplished since using Profit First?

It's nice that every quarter you get this chunk of thousands of dollars that you can use to buy your wife something nice, go on a vacation, etc. Whatever it might be! It makes you feel good that all your hard work is paying off. I've done everything from paying off some credit card debt, getting a really nice barbecue grill for my backyard, and putting money into a vacation account to get us closer to our goals for vacations.

This past winter, my wife and I, and our two kids, ages 18 and 20, went to Italy for about 12 nights. We were in Rome on Christmas, we were in Venice on New Year's Eve, and we had an amazing time!

What advice do you have for another attorney considering Profit First?

For any lawyer considering implementing Profit First, my advice is to just do it. You can afford it. It's a very easy way to get started and what's really exciting about it is that it advises you at the end of every quarter to take what's in that profit account.

Would you recommend this book to another law firm owner?

I would absolutely recommend that all law firm owners read *Profit First for Lawyers*. It provides a very easy-to-understand roadmap on why you *should* and how you *can* obtain financial literacy. When you practice the Profit First methods, you are gaining stability and security, and saving money for yourself in the future.

Printed in the USA
CPSIA information can be obtained
at www.ICGtesting.com
LVHW061219190823
755607LV00008B/232/J